AINTREE IRON

The Autobiography of

Fred and Mercy Rimell

W. H. ALLEN · LONDON
A Howard & Wyndham Company
1977

Printed and bound in Great Britain
by Butler & Tanner Ltd, Frome & London,
for the Publishers, W. H. Allen & Co. Ltd,
44 Hill Street, London W1X 8LB

ISBN 0 491 02350 2

Contents

Acknowledgements

We would like to thank the following for their kind permission to reproduce extracts in this book: Hutchinson Publishing Group Ltd for an extract from *Memoirs of a Racing Journalist* by Sidney Galtrey; *The Observer*; *The Irish Horse*; *The Daily Express*; *The Sunday Times* and *The Sporting Life*.

We would also like to thank Tim Fitzgeorge-Parker for his invaluable help with this book.

I Two on a Horse

Champion jockeys are often asked to name the best ride of their lives. For example Lester Piggott is still stuck on Sir Ivor, despite the obvious claims of Petite Etoile, Crepello and the Triple Crown winner Nijinsky.

Although I was champion National Hunt jockey before and after the war, my best ride was not a racehorse. Not even my champion hurdler, Brains Trust. It was a hunter and I was not alone. I shared the ride with the girl with whom I was to share every aspect of my life, Mercy Cockburn.

It was the winter of 1936. I have always enjoyed life to the full, but it has never been fuller, more exciting or more fun than in those wonderful carefree '30s. When I wasn't riding in races, schooling young horses over fences and hurdles or riding work, I was hunting. So, except in the summer, during daylight I was seldom off a horse for long. And at night? Well, as Whyte Melville described Leicestershire—'Where the business of life is to hunt every day and the nights may take care of themselves as they may!'

Now I was courting Mercy Cockburn from that big, exciting Warwickshire country, a lovely, vivacious dark girl, who was one of the finest of all young horsewomen. She had represented England in France at the age of ten and still has the silver cup that she won there. She'd ridden good point-to-point winners, too, the first when she was only fourteen.

She was the tops on and off a horse. From the day we met at a tennis party in Worcestershire we saw as much as we could of each other.

The kennels of the Croome Foxhounds are close to our home at Kinnersley and I had whipped-in for them when I was twelve years old and Babe Miller was Master. So I knew the hunt and the country really well and I knew that our notorious Bow Brook really took some jumping. That did not stop me trying to negotiate it and frequently succeeding.

On this particular day Mercy, her brother and some friends had come over from the Warwickshire to hunt with us.

It was a great scenting day. Hounds found quickly and were soon running in full cry towards the dreaded brook. The ground was soft and slippery so that the take-offs and landings of the fences were badly poached and one of our older members, George Hunt, a good friend of the Cockburns, sensibly led Mercy and her decent hunter on a way he knew to avoid the brook. Bold as brass and, of course, showing off a bit, I rode hard at it, followed by my future brother-in-law. Inevitably both of us and our horses ended up in the brook. As our mounts galloped off into the distance, we pulled ourselves out, soaked to the skin, cursing because we were missing a hell of a good hunt. I started sprinting after the others, hoping vainly to catch my animal.

Suddenly a horse appeared, galloping towards me. It was Mercy, who was coming back to find me. Fortunately this day she was riding astride. So I leapt up behind her and, clasping her tight round the waist, we set off again after hounds. Faster and faster we went and it suddenly dawned on me that Mercy was having difficulty holding this grand powerful horse. A fence loomed up. We sailed over it and then another. That was spendid. But then I looked over Mercy's shoulder and found we were heading for a five-bar gate. I was scared stiff, but my girl shouted: 'Hang on tight, we'll jump this!' And we did, like a bird. I was chucked up about ten feet in the air, but somehow bounced onto the horse's back again.

The shock really set him off. By now our headlong gallop had carried us to the rest of the hunt and we landed in a lane with deep cart tracks on either side, down which they were all going.

Mercy gasped: 'I can't hold him at all now. My arms have given out.' Faster, faster, faster. Now flat out, we were scattering terrified horses and riders all over the place. With an arm on either side of her I seized hold of the reins, too, and heaved. Every time I pulled, I pushed her forward and every time Mercy tugged, she pushed me back.

It was certainly the best and most exciting ride of my life. We hurtled past the entire field, but, by the time we got to the main road, we had somehow managed to pull up and were able to congratulate each other on a wonderful communal effort.

It has been like that ever since.

II *Newmarket*

I was born at the Kremlin. Not that building with the huge onions that you see in pictures of Moscow, but Kremlin House, Newmarket, the large stable on the Fordham road, where Jeremy Hindley now has his string.

When I came into the world on 24th June 1913 the Guv'nor at the Kremlin was old Joe Butters. My father, Tom Rimell, was his head man.

The Rimells have always been Worcestershire farmers. My grandfather decided that all his four sons, Bob, Dick, Will and Tom, should follow in his footsteps and that he would put them into farms. Tom rebelled. He made up his mind at an early age that he did not want to farm because he had set his heart on becoming a jockey. I don't know where he caught the racing bug, but he had it all right and at fourteen he left home for the Headquarters of Racing, where he served an apprenticeship with a big trainer called Gussey. However, like so many lads, he grew too heavy for the flat and, although he had a few rides over hurdles, he never made the grade as a jockey.

A first-class stableman with a strong personality and a keen sense of discipline, he was soon appointed to one of the top jobs in Newmarket, head man to the famous trainer, Joe Butters, father of a celebrated racing family.

Old Joe finally died in December 1933 at the ripe old age of eighty-six, leaving behind the memory of a cheery, kind-hearted man, who liked to do a good turn to everyone. In all its history Newmarket has never known a more picturesque character. One of my most vivid childhood memories is of the old chap clattering up the High Street, always in a hurry, always answering with a beaming smile the chorused 'Good morning, Mr Butters.'

Ever an early riser, even by the standards of Newmarket, he

remained to the end of his life as spruce and spare as when he had Fred Archer under his care back in the 70s. Joe was a Lancashire lad, born on the Derby family estate of Knowsley, whence presumably stemmed his love of the turf. He served his time with the great John Scott of Malton, Yorkshire, who trained six winners of the Two Thousand Guineas, four of the One Thousand, five of the Derby, nine of the Oaks and no fewer than sixteen of the St Leger, a record that is unlikely ever to be broken.

Many of Scott's classic winners were ridden by his brother, Bill, who had an outsize version of what would today be known as 'a drink problem'. In the latter part of his career he was frequently far too drunk to ride and, if he had not been paralytic, he would have won the 1846 Derby on his own horse, Sir Tatton Sykes. (Jockeys were allowed to own horses in those days.)

Coming south after ending his apprenticeship in the '70s Joe Butters joined one of the most famous trainers of all time, Matthew Dawson, at Newmarket, where Fred Archer was then apprenticed. One day after Archer had ridden a big race winner, the boy received a letter containing a cheque for £100 from the grateful owner. It was his first present. Butters took him down to the bank and made him open an account, thereby starting that carefulness which earned Archer the nickname of 'The Tinman'.

Incidentally, just think of the value of that £100 today, a hundred years later!

Soon afterwards Joe himself accepted a substantial offer to ride in Austria for the Emperor Francis Joseph and several of his court. After thirty years, during which he saw his sons Frank and Fred firmly established as trainers, he returned to Newmarket and turned out hundreds of good winners from Kremlin House.

One year, when my father was head man, they had forty-six two-year-old winners. And there were famous older horses like the eighty-guinea bargain, Mushroom, who won the City and Suburban, top-class condition races, beating mighty Prince Palatine. Then there was a grey called Senseless, whom he bought as a yearling at Doncaster Sales. When his wife exclaimed: 'Joe, what a senseless thing to do!', he called the colt Senseless and won a number of good handicaps with it.

Three years after I was born our stable so nearly won the Derby with a temperamental, excitable colt called Nassovian. Instead of

N. Spear, the stable jockey, who always rode him at home, understood all his peculiarities and had steered him into third place in the Two Thousand, the owner, Sanford, insisted on putting up the crack Franco-American jockey Frank O'Neill in the classic, which was staged at Newmarket during the war.

O'Neill, who had to be brought from New York, never saw his mount until he arrived at Newmarket on Derby Day. He was beaten a neck and a head by Fifinella and Kwang Su.

So Tom Rimell was in the right job and he married Maud Barratt, daughter of one of the town's most important men, the station master. In those days, of course, all horses went by rail from the old station. That is the reason for the extra long platforms. If there was a meeting at, say, Doncaster or York, a racehorse special carrying about fifty horses would leave Newmarket the day before.

All the tack for the stable's runners would be packed up in leather cases of the kind that were used in the old days to carry the jockeys' gear, loaded into the stable trap with all the necessary fodder and everything else, and sent off to the station, where the horses were being led by their stable lads. Actually I think that a lot of racecourses in those days provided free hay, straw and corn for the runners although many of the leading trainers took their own. The horses would probably stay away for two nights.

Of course all the special railway horseboxes, which carried the animals and their lads, had to be scrupulously clean—much cleaner than a first-class British Rail carriage today. My grandfather's job was a very responsible one and he had a large staff to do all the mucking out, setting fair and watering, as well as the many porters customary in those days and the varied maintenance men.

It is fascinating to look back now on a life spent entirely in racing from the very start and to find that it has often come into contact with different aspects of the wider racing scene. For example Joe Butters' son Frank became one of the most successful and most respected trainers of his time. His fourteen classic victories included two Derbys with Mahmoud and Bahram and, in England alone, he won 1,019 races worth £930,000. And his brother, Fred Butters, who was interned in Austria during World War I, won the 1937 Derby with Mid-day Sun.

Frank Butters combined a high degree of professional skill with intense devotion to the interests of his patrons. He believed in giving his horses plenty of work, and those who stood up to his methods came onto the racecourse fit to run for their lives. This he obviously inherited from his father, who also transmitted it to his head man, Tom Rimell.

I did not really like Newmarket. I would never want to train there. Even as a boy, I felt that it was all jealousy and cliques. With the rule of the Jockey Club absolute and all those old trainers in power round the town, it must have been very difficult for a young man to set up there. All those old boys turned out in boots and breeches monopolised the gallops. Each of them had his own little area, where his horses walked around and you had to wait your turn to work a horse. That turn never came until the big trainer had worked all his thirty or forty horses in small batches. You were not permitted to work in between them. And you always had to wait for the big string to move away before you could go in. The atmosphere, dictated from the top, was cold, pompous, oppressive and depressing.

Now that the old boys have gone, the young men have broken through at long last and it must be much more fun training there than ever before.

Most of those exalted old men seemed to believe that nothing mattered except flat racing; that there was no other world of the horse and that no other horses had any value. They regarded jumping with thinly disguised contempt. This was good because it was frequently possible to obtain tremendous bargains from their discards, which in a new life, away from the dull boredom of the 'Blasted Heath' would become star performers as National Hunt horses, polo ponies, point-to-pointers, hunters, show animals, etc.

Notable exceptions were the Leaders. Harvey ('Jack'), a master of hounds, trained Jack Horner to win the 1926 Grand National. And Ted won the big Aintree chase the following year on Sprig. In addition he won the Grand Sefton Chase and Champion Chase twice as well as two Cheltenham Gold Cups, two Imperial Cups and one Champion Hurdle.

Then there were the Collings; and, for all the success and decency of Joe Butters, I knew that my father was delighted to transfer as head man to Bob Colling when that grand old man came down to Newmarket from Yorkshire and settled with his two tall sons, Jack and George, at Bedford Lodge in the Bury Road.

Old Bob had married the daughter of that outstanding professional jump jockey, Bobby I'Anson, about whom George Lambton wrote: 'He was a very tall man, I should say considerably over six foot, but he had an extraordinary knack of tucking himself up on his horse, so that his height looked nothing. No better man over fences and hurdles ever lived, and I think he was the most popular man of his day with the public. There was never a whisper as to his character. We young men worshipped him. He would give us the best advice about riding in the nicest possible way.

'His daughter married Bob Colling, so it was not surprising that her sons, Jack and George, quickly made their mark as jockeys. They inherited not only the skill and character of their grandfather, but also, unfortunately, his length of leg and height, so their riding days were prematurely cut short.'

Both sons, of course, became top-class trainers. I have always liked two of Jack's stories about his father. The first concerned a horse that refused to start in his races while the Collings were still up in Yorkshire and Jack was a jockey.

Old Bob took his son and the reluctant horse on to the gallops, where he gave Jack a leg up, tied a firecracker to the animal's tail, lit the blue touch-paper and stood back. At the first bang the horse hurtled off like a rocket across Middleham Moor. Jack says: 'It was the most terrifying experience. I was quite out of control and, of course, although I knew that there were actually twelve bangs in the firework, I lost count. Just when I was thinking, thank God, it's over at last, bang would go another one and we'd be tearing away again!'

Apparently it did the trick and the horse gave no more trouble at the starting gate.

The other tale which contains a fair lesson arose when Bob first retired and the great old man asked Jack to buy him a yearling. Jack recalls: 'I was terrified of what my father would think of the one I bought him. We had just finished dinner when we were told that the horsebox had arrived from the sales. In fear and trembling I accompanied the old man down to the yard to inspect my selection. He just stood still, saying nothing at all while it was led round and round him. Eventually I could stand it no longer and blurted out: "Well, father, at least you must admit he's a good walker." '

'He replied: "They don't have walking races," turned on his heel and went back to the house.'

But Bob Colling was a grand old boy. He used to drive about in a yellow Rolls Royce which would, I suppose, be worth a small fortune today. He never really conformed to the Newmarket pattern, and with his two sons, spent the winter months hunting with the Newmarket and Thurlow Foxhounds and shooting. He seldom went round the yard to inspect the horses in the evening unless he had owners with him, decentralised splendidly and left virtually everything in the yard to my father. It was a satisfactory arrangement. Dad said: 'I had more trouble keeping their hunters right for Jack and George than managing the stable.'

When my old man went up to see him after evening stables to 'do the list'—arrange the horses and riders for the next morning's exercise—the Guv'nor might say: 'I want to gallop so-and-so and so-and-so.' But my father would reply: 'No, I'm afraid that filly's not pleasing me. She's not feeding very well and we'd better give her a bit of an easy time.' They understood each other and there's no doubt that, by now, Tom Rimell was not just a head man, but as good a trainer as any in the country.

That brilliant future jockey, Harry Wragg, was apprenticed under him with Bob Colling—a fact which later was to stand me in good stead. Apprentices received about half a crown a week and frequently had to do any number of menial jobs like washing out the coal hole.

The standard of smartness and general discipline in and out of stables was far higher than today. For instance, the boys would all be in the saddle room at 3.45 p.m., waiting to be called for evening stables exactly on the stroke of 4 o'clock every afternoon. Outside the entrance of each big Newmarket stable sand would be put down specially and raked, then artistically modelled with the name of the trainer and the date.

Inside everything was spotless. Horses were strapped till they shone sensationally, even if the tiny apprentices had to stand on buckets to reach their heads and the top of their quarters. Litters were always picked up and neatly stacked. The straw carpet was cleanly twisted in at every box door and throughout the place everything that could not be moved was polished or painted.

There were no such things as jodhpurs. All the lads rode out in breeches and leggings. Woe betide the boy who failed to touch his cap and say: 'Good morning, sir,' as he rode past the Guv'nor.

I was in a happy position. The son of a highly respected senior head man and too young to be employed. I didn't go to many race meetings from Newmarket, but then I didn't do any horses either. I used to go up to the stables every evening and go round with my old man.

From the time that I was big enough to be put on a horse's back, I started riding and was soon going out with Bob Colling's string on my pony. Before long I had graduated to a racehorse. There was a little private school, called Mrs Hindle's, which Bill and Fred Rickaby, George Archibald and I attended after we had ridden out first lot.

Horses were tougher in those days and there were many more savages. Mere colts were inclined to attack ponies and hacks. So I had to stay at the rear of the string and keep my pony close to my father on the gallops.

One of the old school of Newmarket trainers, impeccably turned out as usual, was sitting on his beautifully groomed short-tailed cob, serenely contemplating the view as he awaited his string, monarch of all he surveyed, when he was startled by a scream, 'Get out of the bloody way!'

Indignantly and loudly he rebuked the stable lad who had yelled with such gross impertinence, demanding 'D'you know who I am?', only to receive the desperate answer, 'I don't care who the hell you are. You'll be bloody well dead if you don't get out of the way now!' Just in time the trainer realised that the shouting lad was hopelessly out of control on a huge entire colt, who was bearing down on him at a rate of knots with the obvious intention of destroying his hack and, incidentally, himself. He got out of the way!

By the time I was nine years old I was riding fast work. I weighed about 4 st 7 lb. One of the best horses Bob Colling trained was the classic colt Obliterate, who ran in the Derby. His lead horse and galloping companion, Old Wad, was considered a suitable ride for me. But he had a hard mouth and I had no hope of stopping him once he got into his stride. So my father, on his hack, would lead me across the Links and put me upsides with Obliterate. Then we would set off together for a rousing gallop of a mile and a quarter, by the end of which Old Wad had had enough and was happy to pull up.

Meanwhile there was a lot of activity behind the scenes and excitement grew until, when I was eleven years old, my father finally answered the call of his home and announced that we were all going back to Worcestershire, where, with the help of my grandfather and others, he had rented the stables at Kinnersley on the Earl of Coventry's Croome Estate. He had made the grade in racing and had taken the great step of setting up on his own as a trainer.

Even today I can remember his happiness as we said goodbye to Newmarket for good.

III Worcestershire

Worcestershire in the '20s was even more beautiful than it is today. And that's saying something, because I reckon it's the loveliest county in England, steeped in history.

Of course I am biased, but it really has everything that any sportsman and country-lover could desire as well as a magnificent cathedral city with fine architecture, some charming, quaint old streets bearing names like The Shambles and The Tythings, a grand river, a superb cricket ground and old-established quality business of world-wide fame like Lea and Perrins' Worcester Sauce and the Worcester Royal Porcelain Company.

In the rich land between the Cotswolds to the east and the Malvern Hills on the Welsh Borders we have lush pasture land and one of England's greatest fruit gardens, the Vale of Evesham, where, from roadside stalls close to the farms which they serve, you can buy raspberries, strawberries, bundles of delicious asparagus and every other kind of fruit or vegetable.

We have fishing, shooting, hunting, point-to-pointing and racing. Although some of the old courses, like Colwall Park, have disappeared, we are still today surrounded by good meetings. There are Ludlow, Hereford, Wolverhampton, Warwick, Stratford-on-Avon, Chepstow and Worcester itself within easy reach. And Prestbury Park, Cheltenham, the greatest jumping circuit in the world, is only a quarter of an hour away from our home.

The accent is obviously heavily on National Hunt racing, although there are regular flat fixtures at Wolverhampton, Warwick and Chepstow. Worcester, where racing started more than 250 years ago, had a struggle to make the sport pay. The ground frequently became rock hard in the summer, so that there were few runners and very poor quality entertainment. There was no straight sprint course and six furlong races round the home turn sometimes resulted in horses carrying on into the River Severn.

But jumping on this oval track of about 1 mile 5 furlongs, situated between town and river with a splendid outfield, has always been good, except when the Severn used to flood its banks. Then every winter the newspapers would produce their stock picture of swans swimming actually over the tops of the submerged fences with just the circle of the winning post protruding from the water.

The course was closed down during World War II. After it had been refurbished and the fences rebuilt, there was another of the old, familiar flooding periods before the first meeting could be held. People had forgotten the problems during six years of war. The mud had silted up on the fences while they were under water and, when the river subsided, nobody thought to shake it out of the birch and brushwood that formed the obstacles, which, however, looked no different from usual.

Now Worcester had a reputation for nice soft easy fences, so that trainers were inclined to run their slightly chancy jumpers, who could brush right through the top and get away with it.

On this occasion, however, the silted mud had dried and hardened inside the twigs, as the horses discovered to their cost when they hit them. They were jumping stone walls! It was like the Charge of the Light Brigade—horses and riders falling all over the place!

All that flooding trouble has been eliminated now, thanks to the river authorities with their electronic locks and so on. The last flat meeting was held in August 1966. We have grand fences, good ground, a new stand and many other improvements. Even if I were not on the Board, I would always be grateful to have Worcester as my local course.

My favourite racecourse, Cheltenham, naturally features strongly throughout my story. But here I would like to pay tribute to one track that is now defunct and whose passing was the greatest possible tragedy for every true professional in racing—Birmingham.

You saddled in your racecourse stablebox right by the big paddock. The track was perfectly level with well graduated turns and a hurdler or chaser had ample time to see and weigh up the obstacles before he came to them. It was a big galloping course with a straight mile and the draw made no difference at all in the short-distance flat races. The turf, superbly husbanded, stood up to any amount of hard wear. There were no 'ifs' about that track. If the horse was good enough it won. Jumping and flat it was an ideal, fair racecourse, which should have been preserved at all costs. Unhappily it has now been sold for development and the motorway near 'Spaghetti Junction' runs high over the site.

Birmingham is Britain's second biggest city, boasting every kind of industry. Many of the better-off senior business executives, whose homes are in Worcestershire or Warwickshire, are keen sportsmen who love racing and enjoy becoming involved by owning racehorses—a feeling which is shared by Worcestershire's successful sporting farmers, a number of whom breed their own animals.

Yes, there are studs too in our wonderful county, including only a short distance from our home, world-famous Overbury, home of the Holland-Martin family for 250 years, where recently they bred the great dual Derby winner, Grundy.

From the moment that our family arrived at Kinnersley, we were happy as we had never been before.

Father was returning home in triumph. He had proved his point. Starting right at the bottom of the racing industry, he had gone right through it. Now he was ready to reap the rewards.

Ben Roberts had been training at Kinnersley. My old man gave him some money to persuade him to move out and he went to Bishop's Cleeve above Cheltenham.

The M5 motorway now divides us from our gallops and schooling fences in Old Park, but in those pre-war days it had not even been thought of. In the parkland of the Croome Estate we have always had every variety of scenery, ground and gradient to keep horses fit and interested.

The wide, bleak expanse of Newmarket Heath is obviously right for the flat, otherwise so many great champions would not have been trained there throughout history. But these are almost invariably young stock. And I will always remain convinced that older animals, like jumpers, need to maintain their spark and interest with trees and hills whose gradients also put muscle in the right places.

From the moment that I first saw it over fifty years ago, the house by the road in the straggling little Worcestershire village of Kinnersley has been home.

At first my elder sister Vera and I were taken aback. We had been brought up thinking of training establishments as the large, somewhat pretentious yards at Newmarket and trainers' 'residences' (I think that's the only word to describe them!) as grandiose affairs way beyond our reach.

Our new home was perfect. A thoroughly comfortable, solidly built brick and stone country house, small enough to be cosy and warm, yet large enough to accommodate a farmer of means or the agent to a large estate.

In a way it's like a farmhouse, because, as you enter the wide gates, the house is immediately on the left of the drive and the yard on the right, so that you live on the premises and are totally involved, as a professional trainer should be.

We have since heightened this involvement by building beside the house, looking into the yard, a light comfortable office, where we can work efficiently and make plans and where, on Sunday mornings, we usually crack a few bottles of champagne with visiting friends and owners.

Owners are often held to be the bane of a trainer's life.

My father and I have been very lucky in our patrons. With very few exceptions, I get on well with all sorts. Whenever you see an owner constantly changing his trainer, it is quite safe to assume that the fault's with the former and not with the latter.

A trainer is not unlike a master of foxhounds, standing on a hill for everyone to throw mud at. Most men in other walks of life enjoy immunity from slander. So does the trainer, as long as his often thankless efforts are successful.

But wait till things go at all wrong, as they inevitably will in a job where the basic ingredient consists of delicate expensive highly-strung live animals.

The trouble with many owners, particularly those who have recently come into the game, is that they listen too much to the tittle-tattle of the friendly busybodies who are attracted to them like wasps to a jam jar. Some owners make up their minds that their horse is sure to win a particular race and, heedless of their trainer's warnings, tell all their friends to back the animal. So, when the trainer's forebodings are proved correct (they should be—he lives with the horse!) and the horse is beaten, those great sporting chaps, the owner's friends, who have 'done their dough', must find a scapegoat. They don't pay any part of the horse's keep and bear none of the responsibility but, talking now through their pockets and smarting under the reverse in their fortunes, they assume a proprietorial interest.

As Al Read would say, 'You've 'eard 'em!'

'The jockey rode a shocking race . . . If he was "off", which I doubt (I've heard some funny things about him lately), the horse wasn't . . . Short of work? I couldn't believe how much extra weight he was carrying when I saw him in the paddock. They must have been feeding him Christmas puddings. And he nearly blew the stand down afterwards . . . I wonder what the trainer is keeping him for. He certainly wasn't busy today . . . Why did the trainer run him on that ground? It obviously doesn't suit him. Wouldn't be surprised if he'd broken him down, when not "having a go" . . . Course, he was so bloody easy to back, we ought to have suspected something. These bookies know the score alright. I took 9 to 2 and the next thing I hear is 6 to 1. I ask you . . . ! The stewards must have been blind, drunk or blind-drunk, or they'd have had them in and asked some very searching questions. If I'd been a steward, the trainer's feet wouldn't have touched the ground. He'd have been straight in and up to Portman Square . . . It'ud be better if he had his horses "off" as often as he had it off with little Lily. They say no stable girl is safe in Newmarket. Wouldn't be surprised if it's apprentices, too . . . ! Couldn't train ivy up a wall!' etc. etc.

Mind, days before a race the trainer told the owner that his horse was not really good enough for what was expected of him. And the trainer, who loves his horses, is proud of the brave showing that his charge has made, even though out-classed. He thinks the jockey has given the horse a grand ride, too. But the one thing these people will never take into account is that the horse might not be good enough.

All this hostile comment, produced very knowingly from gents wearing huge long binoculars, is dinned into the ears of the owner who, knowing very little about the game, is inclined to think that there is something in what has been said. Everyone knows that shady things have happened on the turf in the past and the newcomer is soon induced to suspect that he has fallen into a den of thieves. Some of the mud has stuck, and, in the end, the trainer is the chief sufferer. If the owners had less confidence in their friends and more faith in the honesty and ability of their trainers, they would be far happier and life would be more pleasant for those they employ. It is all too easy to underestimate the amount of mischief which these busybodies can cause.

A trainer friend of my father's had an animal entered in a decent selling hurdle. He wanted to sell it because it made a noise and was rapidly getting worse. On the morning of the race the owner, an old friend, telephoned to say that he could not come to the meeting, but should he back the horse? As he was a very small bettor, the trainer said he thought it had a good chance, but he should have only a moderate bet because it had not been doing too well lately. He suggested a 'pony', adding that the owner would be well rid of it if it won.

In those days the seller was the first race on the card. My father's friend was held up with a puncture on his way to the races and just managed to get to the course as the runners left the start. He had been unable to tell his head man to run the horse in blinkers nor had he been able to give riding instructions to his jockey. As a result he had no bet. Fortunately everything worked out all right. The horse won quite comfortably and was well sold at the subsequent auction. That night the owner telephoned to say that he had had his 'pony' on and was very pleased at winning. The trainer had learned incidentally that just before the start a big professional backer had a substantial bet on the horse which caused him to shorten quickly in price.

The following day the owner was in his London club, where he was congratulated by a friend on having won. 'You must have had a real good touch,' he said. The owner replied that he had only invested a 'pony' and that his trainer did not have a bet at all, having failed to arrive on the course in time.

'Rubbish!' replied the other member. 'He had a very big bet at S.P., and that was why he didn't turn up until too late.' The owner told him he was wrong, but Mr Busybody, instead of saying that he must have been misinformed, stuck to his story, insisting that his statement was correct for he knew just how the S.P. was worked.

A few days later my father's friend heard the story from his owner, who was staying the weekend with him. However hard he questioned, the name of the busybody was not divulged. 'I'm much too fond of you to allow you to be charged with murder!' said his friend.

This little incident shows how many difficulties trainers have to contend with apart from training winners, which is quite a hard enough problem, as we all know!

In general the type of owner in British racing has changed considerably during the last half century. Owing to high taxation, death duties, estate duty, and all the various other little imposts which successive governments have been able to produce for the persecution of the long-suffering British public, a great number of those good sportsmen who have been brought up in the world of hunting, racing, and all country pursuits have disappeared as owners. Such owners who really understand racing and know that a horse is not a machine are indeed a pleasure to work and train for. Naturally their places have been taken, but in a great many cases their successors have not been lucky enough to grow up in the game. Some of them cannot understand that, even if they have paid a large sum for a horse, it need not necessarily turn out to be a star. The trainer with owners who understand the facts of life is a lucky man. His patrons will take the rough with the smooth, victory with defeat. But the owner who goes in for racing knowing nothing about it, regarding horses as mere machines that will pop up and win whenever required to do so, is going to be a nuisance. Such owners, who race only for money, are always difficult to deal with, always ready to listen to the busybodies in their clubs.

A little knowledge is as dangerous in horse racing as in any other walk of life. And the owner with a little knowledge can do a lot of harm by his ill-timed interference. To be a successful owner a man must have implicit confidence in his trainer. If a newcomer to the game wishes to interfere he would be much better advised to appoint a manager who knows the business inside out and let him act for him. Such a man could keep both owner and trainer happy, but unfortunately he is a very rare breed indeed. On the other hand, if the owner knows as much about racing horses as he seems to think, he would be a great deal wiser if he took over some stables and trained his own horses.

It is very exasperating for a trainer to receive advice from someone who has never trained a horse and who derives his scanty knowledge from what he overhears in the smoking-room of his club. Some years ago an owner of this type had two bays at Kinnersley, one of which was a very well-known eight-year-old and the other his three-year-old half-brother, whom he had bought himself and who was of little account. Nevertheless the owner had decided that he was to become a great horse. To soften the blow, my father told him that he was very backward, which was quite true, for he would certainly not win races as a three or four-year-old.

When the owner came to look at his ewe lamb, he found himself by mistake in the box occupied by the poor creature's distinguished brother, who had won many races in a deservedly publicised career. He looked this splendid animal up and down very knowingly, patted its neck and congratulated the lad, finally saying to my father, 'I quite agree with you. He is backward. He wants time. He will never be any good until next season at the earliest.' Unfortunately for him the younger horse never was any good and indeed never won a race of any kind.

I have always been lucky in having generous owners, but there are owners who are 'slow parters'. People who lavish large ostentatious tips on head waiters are somehow apt to be particularly mean in the privacy of training stables about giving presents to the stable lads who work hard in all weathers to look after and care for their expensive charges. They are ignorant of the good that a little encouragement can do and of the indisputable fact that contented lads are one of the most vital ingredients in the production of successful horses. I am glad to say that the Jockey Club, in their wisdom, have finally taken steps to frustrate owners of racehorses who are unduly slow in paying their training bills—the bane of many trainers, particularly today when the cost of everything involved in training, forage, fuel, electricity, transport, labour, etc. has risen so astronomically.

But, as I say, we have always been very lucky on the whole with our patrons at Kinnersley. When he started training in the '20s, my father's owners included his brother, always known as 'W.J.', Gordon Orr; Lord Glanely, the famous shipping magnate; Bill Parsonage, the Ludlow bookmaker, who won the National with Forbra; Arthur Hesketh, who had that good old mare Song Of Love; Lady Barbara Smith, for whom he trained Dictum and that splendid family of horses; Major Harold Rushton, the top-class amateur and point-to-point rider and Sir Edward Hanmer, who had horses here for more than fifty years until his death at the start of 1977. Nobody except my old man and I ever trained jumpers for Sir Edward, and you can imagine my great pride when I was able to win the 1976 Cheltenham Gold Cup for him with Royal Frolic. This was his greatest moment as an owner.

His death was a great shock as he was a personal friend to me. Not only had my father trained for him, but I had ridden for Sir Edward. He was one of racing's best known figures. Born at Bettisfield Park, Whitchurch in Shropshire, he had a rich sporting background but racing was always his favourite sport. He was Master of the Watkin-Wynn Hunt from 1946 to 1953, bred bloodstock on his home farm and had a fair success with them. Money Box won the Manchester Cup, and other horses to carry his colours with distinction were Fury, who won the fillies' St Leger, the Park Hill Stakes; Pomagne, winner of the Cumberland Plate; Dumpy, who won a number of races in the '60s and Teme Willow, with whom I won the National Hunt Handicap Chase at Cheltenham's Festival Meeting in two successive years.

The late Dobson Peacock, that great Northern trainer, had charge of Sir Edward's flat horses and in 1931 felt confident that he would achieve the ambition of Sir Edward's life with Gallinin in the Derby, but the colt was found to be lame at Epsom, having been pricked while being plated. The plates were removed and exercise shoes were substituted. Gallinin made all the running but he lost his off fore shoe at the bottom of the hill after Tattenham Corner and, although lame, still managed to finish fifth. Dick Peacock carried on training Sir Edward's horses on the flat in the tradition of his grandfather.

Sir Edward's first appointment as a steward was at Haydock in 1929. Thereafter he was associated with many race meetings as a steward or director and until his retirement at seventy-five he acted as steward at Haydock, Wolverhampton, Chester, York, Ludlow, Bangor-on-Dee, Uttoxeter and at one of the Newmarket meetings.

Shortly before he died I was able to tell him that his nice young jumper Royal Gaye had won impressively over hurdles. I am happy to say that Lady Hanmer proposes to keep the family horses with us.

My father had started at the bottom of the tree and gone right up the racing ladder learning all the time. So, from the moment he started at Kinnersley he was very successful. He was an outstanding horseman and whenever there was a difficult customer he would get up on it and organise it himself. He used to ride gallops for quite a while. He was very hard on his horses and gave them an awful lot of work. But he fed them well—really well. He said, 'If they'd eat gold, I'd give it to them!'

I suppose the answer was that he was a very good stable man and a first-class feeder. He would give them glucose and any other additives that he thought they needed. But, my word, they had to work for their keep. We would take horses from Kinnersley to Strensham, work them there and come back which would take at least three hours. And they had to gallop the full two miles. Those that survived went on and the others fell by the wayside, never to be heard of again. These were not just ordinary gallops but proper trials when the jockeys weighed out and the horses carried lead in weight cloths. The survivors were real tough animals. In those days a good flat racehorse was considered too high-class to go jumping. Unlike today it was unthinkable for a decent middle-distance animal on the flat to be turned to hurdling. Sometimes the odd sprinter that was past his best might be turned to hurdles, but never your mile or mile and a quarter horse. Let there be no mistake, they were fitter and stronger animals in those days.

Over the years they have bred for speed, speed and still more speed so that eventually it has come out in the jumpers who now come from the flat. We hate horrible, spindly-legged little beasts, which is why Mercy and I have to keep going over to Ireland because there they have kept more of the old, original National Hunt type of horse. They stick to their old jump families and give the produce time to mature. Of course some French horses have made the grade, but they are very much the exception to the rule. Fortina and Mandarin come immediately to mind, but, as far as I can remember, the only French horse that had the necessary bone was Mont Tremblant whom Fulke Walwyn trained for

Dorothy Paget. He had the physique to cope with normal jumping going and to carry the weight. So many of these recruits from the flat have not the physique either to cope with normal winter ground or to carry the weights. Breeding a National Hunt horse involves such a long-term policy. It is a six-year project. Very few people today can afford it. The last Englishman to do it successfully was Harry Dufossee who was the shining example of breeding the National Hunt horse. Edward Courage, too, has had a wonderful run.

From the moment that my father took out a training licence at Kinnersley he started saddling winners. Most of these were jumpers but he had a number of flat horses too and indentured me to himself as an apprentice. During the winter I would hunt with the Croome Foxhounds and, at the age of twelve, I actually whipped in to them. So, although I was riding as a jockey on the flat, I had already got the bug. When I was hunting I was jumping all the time and I knew what my future would be. In the meantime I was going to make the most of my opportunities while I was light enough and determined to learn all I could and to make as much money as possible by riding on the flat. It was a great education. Appropriately it was my grandfather who gave me my first winner.

The old man still lived in the family home at Leigh near Worcester. Although he had never owned many racehorses, he had a few years earlier bought a brood mare called Revolie with a foal at foot. Rowlie, as the foal was called, grew into a useful horse, whom my father trained to win a number of decent hurdle races and who was considered fast enough to be entered for a one and a half mile apprentice race at Chepstow's opening meeting.

Although I was only twelve years old, I had already had one ride in public on a mare called Fouration at Nottingham and had quickly realised that I had nothing to fear from the other apprentice riders, who were mostly older than I. Very much the opposite in fact. My experience on Newmarket Heath and in the hunting field had given me confidence in my own ability to handle a horse. I think they were more frightened of me than I was of them.

Chepstow was to become one of my favourite racecourses. Now, thanks to the motorway and the Severn Road Bridge, which takes us virtually from door to door, it is very much a local fixture for us at Kinnersley. In 1926, however, it was quite a trek for the entire Rimell family. It was a memorable day for us and for those who had conceived and constructed the track. Chief among these were our owners Lord Glanely, Mrs Mundy, W. R. Lysaght and R. E. More. All were keen racing enthusiasts and all had thought big. I have never bothered about the argument whether Monmouthshire is in Wales or England. Suffice to say here that Glanely and his fellow directors laid out an immense amount of money on the new course, confident that it would draw the huge sporting urban population of Cardiff and Swansea. Unfortunately their dream has not been realised until now when the improved roads have made it so much more accessible. The big stands, the beautiful setting, the size of the course itself and the vast crowd on that opening day made it an awe-inspiring prospect for a twelve-year-old.

Chepstow is situated in four hundred acres of glorious parkland only a mile from the Severn Bridge where the Wye Valley runs into the Severn estuary. It is left-handed and caters for jumping and flat racing. About two miles round, it undulates sharply, though this does not seem to affect a long-striding animal as might be expected. In fact, I have won races here with many horses of this type. The switchback straight seems to appeal to most horses. There is a straight mile and all races up to this distance are run over it. Downhill until about half way, it rises sharply for two furlongs and then ends up with another slight downhill slant to the winning post. Races on the round course join the straight just after the five-furlong marker. The bends are easy and the run-in on the jumping course is about 250 yards. You need a horse with plenty of stamina to win if the going is at all heavy. I had that sort of horse. My father said: 'He's a good stayer. Kick him in the belly and keep going.' I did just that and won by eight lengths in a canter. Although my father was obviously very proud as I pulled up and came back to unsaddle, he was never one to show excessive enthusiasm. He just smiled and said: 'Well done, son!' But my grandfather was over the moon. He kept repeating: 'I owns him, me son trains, and me grandson rode him.'

As for me, I knew that I was on my way at an age when most boys were still at school. I have always derived great satisfaction in later years when reading that Lester Piggott rode his first winner at the age of eleven. I rode mine just one year later. Before we returned to Chepstow I had several rides on other courses, but did not again 'trouble the judge' as the more fanciful scribes have it. Now I was to learn what riding on the flat really meant when I was in competition with the great jockeys who rode in this country between the wars.

IV The Flat

There were two horses 'trained T. R. Rimell' in the same race on my second visit to Chepstow. This was not a contest confined to apprentices like the previous race, but an open one in which I would be taking on the senior jockeys. I was to ride the mare Fouration and Michael Beary, who was my father's stable jockey at the time, was on the more fancied of the pair.

Michael was a voluble and engaging Irishman from Tipperary, a leprechaun with a sort of native cunning and a great affinity for horses. He had served his apprenticeship at Chattis Hill, Stockbridge with Atty Persse of The Tetrarch fame and owed his start in life to Atty's long-time stable jockey, Steve Donoghue, rider of The Spotted Wonder. The legendary little man, 'Come on, Steve!', who steered six Derby winners, recognised the Irish boy's potential and, unbeknown to the Guv'nor, took him off to nearby Salisbury and put him on a winner.

I consider myself lucky to have known Steve, and when he died quite suddenly in 1945 I, like everyone in racing, felt that I had lost a friend. A native of Cheshire despite his name, he was a superb horseman with beautiful hands and it was sheer joy to watch him cantering down to the start on a highly strung two-year-old, gentling it on the longest possible rein. He genuinely loved horses and they took kindly to him. Steve kept his iron nerve to the end, despite some dreadful falls. After a shattering crash in the 1920 Derby on very hard ground, when he lay prone in the path of the oncoming field, he walked back to the weighing room and rode two more winners that afternoon.

Sir Gordon Richards has said: 'Steve had this uncanny instinct whereby he would ride into a wall of horses and an opening would always suddenly appear for him.'

He was at his brilliant best at Epsom and the popular belief was that he invariably had one leg over the rails as he rode round Tattenham Corner. At a time when there were no television or pop stars and movies were in their infancy, Steve was an idol.

A little short-legged man with a husky voice and a charming smile, he had a most attractive personality and was a great favourite with the opposite sex, numbering several titled ladies among his most intimate friends. He was kind and generous—indeed too generous for his own good—and even at the height of his popularity, he never became swollen-headed or overbearing. Sometimes he was deplorably casual to those who employed him, but his charm usually extricated him from the more awkward situations. He won fourteen English classics, four Irish Derbys and two Grand Prix de Paris. Steve's last big triumph was on Exhibitionist in the Oaks of 1937.

Atty Persse, who knew him better than anyone, told my father that he rated Steve the greatest jockey of all time.

Michael Beary modelled himself on his mentor and guide with fair success, but in some respects he was a caricature of Donoghue. At his best—and consistency was hardly one of his greatest virtues—the foxy-faced Irishman was a top-class jockey, a stylist who was often brilliant with difficult horses. His great trouble throughout his life was his own unequable temperament and an overabundant self-confidence that at times could be extremely irritating.

Five years before the war the late Sidney Galtrey ('Hotspur' of the *Daily Telegraph*), wrote:

> There is no more ardent believer in Michael Beary than himself. Self-confidence, asserted within limits, may be helpful in a hard and highly competitive world. Beyond those limits there can be danger. Yet they are never very apparent to Michael Beary, or, if they are, he takes a chance. He is an unusual Irishman, though not in his knowledge of the thoroughbred, which goes much deeper than with most jockeys. If you would know anything of breeding, make and shape, and of the secrets of race-riding, by all means apply to him and they will be revealed. He is not the dove of peace and tranquility when waters are ruffled on the turf. One gets the notion that he never likes to be out of it if there is any ruffling to be done. The politics of the turf are like

as a Bible is to some people. They bring him much peace of mind. He is at once the reformer and the revolutionist.

As a rider he has style and perfect hands. He is wide-awake at the starter's end, and if he can win with 7 lbs or 10 lbs in hand, without letting us be aware of the fact, he would be immensely pleased. Those few pounds, he argues, might come in so very useful on another occasion. He has read of the tricks of Archer and Fordham of old and seeks to blend them. But it is not unimportant to bear in mind that races in their day were vastly differently run to the races of modern times. Then they dawdled. Now they race. So the jockey who schemes to cut things fine may one day find himself assailed when an assault is not expected. In such circumstances a horse is given a hard race when it should have had an easy one, with always the possibility of tragedy lurking.

Michael Beary has not been well served for one of such proved ability. As the Aga Khan's first jockey he could have ridden Blenheim when that horse won the Derby of 1930. He favoured riding Rustom Pasha, who was unplaced. Again in the St Leger of 1932, when the Aga Khan had four runners, his choice was Dastur, who, however, was beaten a neck by the stable companion, Firdaussi. Any other jockey would probably have chosen the same. Somehow other jockeys are never singled out to be the playthings of a capricious Fate. He is gifted, and at times his riding excites the greatest admiration. A hard worker with Hitler-like tendencies.

Michael was a great man to hounds and rode several steeplechase winners. He had a rather whining Irish voice, but could exert the charm when he wanted to. Although he never enjoyed Steve's phenomenal success with the ladies, he had his moments, during one of which he married Eve, a young lady of excellent family, who was subsequently a popular, hardworking, and highly respected member of the English racing press.

In a typical burst of generous sympathy for one of Michael's lean periods Sir Gordon Richards, the champion who had yet to win the Derby, gave him the ride in 1937 on Mid-day Sun whom Beary steered to victory first in the Lingfield Derby Trial and then in the Derby at Epsom.

On the gallops Michael, as stable jockey, would order us boys about: 'Come up a little. Don't hang back!' 'Pull him back to me now. You're riding work, not trying to win the gallop!'—and so on.

My father told me how Michael, when first jockey to his old Guv'nor, was riding in the Victoria Cup on one of the rare occasions when a Persse apprentice had a ride on a fancied horse. As the starter called them up, the lad brought his mount into line beside the great man only to be told by Michael in that high-pitched Irish drawl: 'This is no place for you, little boy. It's very dangerous. Get back out of it, do you hear what I say? Get back!' Accustomed as he was to obeying Michael's orders, the boy pulled back. At that moment the tapes went up and he was hopelessly left. That danger was out of the way.

On a sunny summer afternoon Michael and I, dressed in our shiny white silk colours, walked into the Chepstow paddock with the other jockeys. We went up to my father and touched our hats. 'Michael', he said, 'I want you to look after my boy, tell him what he ought to do and make sure he's all right at the starting gate. Take care of him now. He's only ridden one winner.'

Then, while Michael was busy chatting up the owners, my father took me out of earshot and said: 'Now don't take any notice of Michael, son. He'd kid a duck of its nest. You jump that mare out of the gate and rattle her along for three furlongs, sit against her for a while and then make the best of your way home. I think you've got a very good chance.'

On the way to the start Michael knowingly and confidentially, in the manner of a master teaching his favourite pupil, gave me instructions which were exactly opposite my father's on how to ride the Chepstow five furlongs. 'Look here my boy,' he said. 'Just let that mare of yours canter along quietly for the first two furlongs. Then, when she's got on her legs properly, let her run along for the last three.'

Michael's horse was the odds-on favourite, but I won. I obeyed my father's instructions and I won. I was so delighted with my second winner that, when I got back to the weighing room, and Harry Wragg said: 'Well done, son!' I couldn't keep my mouth shut and told Harry about the two different instructions that I had received. As he was such a friend of the family, I told him what the old man had said and that Michael had instructed me just to let the mare canter along for the first two furlongs. Harry told the other jockeys and they pulled Michael's leg unmercifully. They gave him such hell that he would not speak to me for about a month afterwards.

Harry, eleven years my senior, was already a first-class jockey. A strong character, utterly dedicated and ambitious, he combined method with style and would always keep a horse beautifully balanced. Even in that vintage period he stood out as one of the coolest, most calculating jockeys ever but, in direct contrast to Beary, he was always ready to help a youngster.

So too, of course, was Sir Gordon Richards, who had won the first of his twenty-five championships in the year before I rode my first winner. Then, as now, he has always been a wonderful person, a grand chap ever ready to help anyone. With his brilliance at the gate, his intense will to win and his immensely powerful unorthodox loose rein and sideways-sitting, whip-swinging style, he was a terribly hard man to beat. Chepstow was one of Gordon's happy hunting grounds. It was here that he won eleven of the twelve races at a two-day meeting and was only narrowly beaten in the last.

In all I rode thirty-four winners on the flat. My best meeting was Worcester, where I rode four of my father's five winners in the two-days. My great friend Willie Stephenson, a first-class lightweight jockey, rode the other. Since he gave up riding Willie has become one of the only trainers to win both the Derby and the Grand National—with Arctic Prince and Oxo. We used to travel nearly everywhere by train to ride at the various race meetings. When he first got going Willie always used to wear a bowler hat. One day I threw it out of the train.

It was strange in view of what was to happen later but Liverpool was my bogey course as a jockey. It had a sort of hoodoo for me. I never rode a winner there either on the level or over obstacles. The best horse I ever rode on the flat, Promptitude, trained by my father, won the Redcar Handicap for me but I was beaten on him in two Liverpool Cups—first by Johnny Dines, who beat me by a head and next by that grand jockey Freddy Fox, a man of intelligence, skill and infinite kindness. The following year I could not do the weight. Willie rode the horse and won. He also had the mount when Promptitude won the Manchester November Handicap in 1929 at 33 to 1. But by that time there was no way that I could have possibly ridden at 6 st 13 lbs!

It was different riding on the flat then from today. We were very much regimented by the old-time jockeys. Lester Piggott found the same thing when he started riding after the war and ascribes a great deal of the troubles that he got into to that very thing. His explanation is typically simple: 'Old jockeys riding for old trainers and old stewards.'

In life there is always bitter resentment from moderate people who have enjoyed success against the upsurge of brilliant youth. Actors and actresses will use their experience to upstage young members of their profession, frequently with devastating effect.

Between the wars the jockeys, many of whom were to resent young Lester when hostilities ceased and racing really got going, were in their prime and really well entrenched. Brownie Carslake, who was to die from excessive wasting at that age of fifty-five in 1941, was one of the worst.

Tall for a flat-race jockey, dark and somewhat saturnine, Bernard Carslake, popularly known as 'Brownie', was one of the best and most stylish of the many good Australian jockeys who have ridden in England. Before the first war he rode successfully in Austria and Hungary, moving on the outbreak of war in 1914 to Rumania and thence to Russia. He escaped with difficulty during the Revolution arriving in England penniless in 1917.

He was a particularly powerful finisher and, with his long legs, a wonderful rider of a two-year-old. But he was a dour, morose sort of chap with a strong sense of his own importance.

One day Major Beatty had three runners in a race at Derby over one and a half miles. Willie Stephenson rode one, I rode another and Henry Wragg was on the one that was fancied. We were told to jump off and make a good gallop of it. I lasted the longest and was still in front when we turned into the straight and I heard somebody shouting. It was Brownie Carslake; he was trying to come up on my inside. So I went straight back into the fence, closed the gap and stopped him immediately. When he eventually got out, he came by me screaming and shouting and nearly put me over the rails. Harry Wragg duly won on our fancied runner and I had obviously done a good job. But Carslake reported me to the stewards in such violent terms that they at first decided to refer the matter to the stewards of the Jockey Club in London. This was the worst thing that could possibly happen to a young jockey at the start of his career and the tough Australian knew it. But he was determined to get his pound of flesh. However, by the time the stewards had sorted the case out properly, Harry Wragg and the other jockeys had given Carslake such a hell of a rocket that the case was dropped and I was merely cautioned. That was my first appearance in the stewards' room and I was furious about it. I went straight to Carslake, looked into that lean dark face with its hooked nose and said: 'Just you wait. One of these days I'll be as big as you are.' I harboured that resentment for a long time and I kept my word.

Some time later he was riding for my father at Worcester and, after he had weighed out, Carslake gave me the saddle. I threw it back at him and said: 'You take it out yourself!' and walked out of the weighing room.

I finally got my revenge one day many years later at Liverpool. On Grand National day the card traditionally started with a hurdle race but, apart from that and the big chase all other events were on the flat. There were separate changing rooms and it has always been amusing to notice the difference in size and build of the two types of jockeys. There is always a bit of tension before the National, but I was young, strong, supremely fit and looking forward to my ride. I was talking and laughing with Gerry Wilson and I said: 'You know today is the day to go and tell that bloody old Carslake that I am just about ready for him.'

So I went into the flat room and squared up to Carslake, looking pretty tough. I said: 'Now then you old bugger, do you remember what I said to you seven years ago? You were always bullying me as a kid and once did your best to wreck my career. Now it's time I got my own back and sorted you out. What about it, eh?'

Carslake did not know what to say. So, of course, I started to laugh. But he still did not see the joke. Anyone else would have laughed with me, shaken hands and buried the hatchet. But not Brownie. He was like a sour old prima donna. But, my word, he was a good rider. He and Joe Childs were the two best long distance I'd ever seen. Both of them were outstanding, super horsemen with beautiful hands. But Childs was a different cup of tea.

Although in his early days he had such a fiery temper that young jockeys were terrified of him, he had mellowed with age by the time that I was riding and, immensely proud of being the Royal jockey, was universally popular. He was one of the all-time greats. Tall, strong and exceptionally patient, he excelled at riding a waiting race. He won fifteen classics including three Derbys and when he won the Triple Crown with Gainsborough in 1918 on riding leave from the 4th Hussars, he gave all his fees and presents to regimental funds.

If the professionals were outstanding, the amateurs were nearly as good. I remember particularly Jack Fawcus, Peter Payne-Gallwey and Ginger Whitfield.

All the time that I had been riding on the flat I had also been hunting and schooling over fences and hurdles, so that when inevitably I got too heavy at the age of eighteen I was ready for my real job in life. But I never regretted those flat-racing years. They taught me so much that was to be vitally useful in later life, both as a jockey and then as a trainer.

V The Real Thing

I took out a jumping licence in 1930 and I rode my first winner over hurdles at Cheltenham on Southam owned by Mrs Gresham and trained by my father.

From the moment that I went into the changing room I knew I was among friends. Even though I was still only a kid, I shared the camaradarie of the jumping jockeys. In those prewar days money was short and we got only £3 a ride. We used to joke about a pound a mile. The racecourses were not very well looked after and many of the fences were stiffer, blacker and much straighter than they are now. But there was not so much racing and every jockey was keener to ride whatever came along.

There were not so many runners in a race and you knew your jockeys better. There were fewer boys and such as there were—I was one myself—were bloody well frightened into going straight. So on the whole it was easier to ride a race than it is today when half these barbarians don't know where the hell they're going.

You knew where you were going and you knew where to go. There was a much better spirit in the changing room than there is today. All the jockeys were always fooling about and laughing. But there was no quarter shown when you went out on the course.

Speck and Stott were two of the best riders, particularly over fences, I have ever known. Quite exceptional. And there were flat-race jockeys riding over hurdles and fences, like Frank Wootton before them and Johnny Gilbert after.

Then there were George Pellerin, Staff Ingham and Harry Sprague over hurdles. There were some wonderful amateurs too, like Jack Fawcus, Perry Harding, Fred Thackeray and Sandy Scratchley. And there was still the great Rees, the grand old man ruling the weighing room. I remember as a kid being sent out to get the scotch for him before a race. You would never think of trying to come up on their inside. In general racing was not as straight as it is today. Horses were kept and put by for races. Big gambles were brought off. There were no sponsored races and the prize money was so low that the money had to come from somewhere. So they gambled. To give you an example, when they finally altered the conditions of the Grand National in 1932, the year my father won the race with Forbra, qualification was confined to horses who 'at the time of entry' had been placed in a steeplechase of not less than three miles and worth at least £200 to the winner or in a steeplechase of any distance at Aintree.

There is not the heavy gambling today. Even if the modern bookmakers would stand it (which they wouldn't!), the stake money has improved so much in recent years that there is not the urgent need for big gambles. Very few horses run today that are not fancied. Most animals that are capable of winning on the day do so because of the stake money and the high cost of keeping a horse. Of course there is the odd handicap like the Schweppes Gold Trophy, where some people will try to get their horses handicapped. But by and large, I should think that there are fewer non-triers in jumping now than there have ever been. If you run a horse down the course for several outings, you will probably find that on the day when you really want him to win you get beaten by some unconsidered small permit holder. Jump racing was much smaller then. There were no trainers with seventy or eighty horse strings. Mostly the bigger men had about thirty-five to forty. But there is no doubt that it was far more sporting and was fun in those days.

In those early days the horse would walk from Kinnersley to Defford, a distance of about four miles, and the luggage would go in a pony and trap to the station. It would be nothing for the horses and lads to be coming back home at nine o'clock in the dark of a winter's night. £3 a ride, a fiver a winner and no travelling expenses. One day at Newton Abbot I asked Danny Morgan in the weighing room how many rides he had at the meeting. He said: 'Oh, only one.' It was a three mile chase—a pound a mile—and it fell!

I rode twenty-eight winners that first season, all over hurdles. Indeed by April 1932 I still had not ridden over fences and so missed the ride on our own Grand National winner Forbra.

I mentioned that in this year the conditions for the National had been altered. But moderate horses could still qualify because even then steeplechases of three miles were often contested by small fields, especially in bad weather or during the early months of the season. So a horse had only to finish 'last of three' to be placed and so qualify for Liverpool. Furthermore the qualifications did not have to be recent. A horse who had finished last of three at the age of five was still eligible for the National eight years later.

But Forbra was a good tough horse whom my father had schooled well. He was owned by the Ludlow bookmaker Bill Parsonage, who had bought him for 1,500 guineas from Mrs Hunt of Rutland, who had found him too slow for flat racing. He was a fine strong horse who had taken well to jumping and my father had schooled him splendidly. But he was only seven years old and a virtual novice.

Nowadays a horse that has not won a race remains a novice for the whole of that season and can thus compete in novice races. But this is only a recent development. Before a horse was a novice for only a month after winning its first race. Thereafter he had to take on the experienced horses in open events and was usually at a considerable disadvantage. It is one thing to jump at racing speed upsides with novices like yourself but quite another to have to take on those who have learnt all the tricks of the trade.

Now Bill Parsonage and my father were aiming for a nice touch in a big novice chase at Newbury. As a preliminary, they gave Forbra an outing at Taunton. It was a three mile chase and he was not supposed to be trying, just having a run. But the best-laid plans are apt to go wrong and he won. So the gamble had gone astray and he would have only one more novice chase—at Newbury. But he had qualified for the National by winning that race. Now his novice days were limited after his Taunton victory. So they ran him at Newbury and he finished second but the winner was disqualified and he was awarded the race. He was finished as a novice and so they decided that despite his age they would let him have a go at Aintree because he was a first-class jumper and a really good stayer. He was known as 'the horse that couldn't fall' and the Cheltenham jockey Rex Hamey was booked by my father to ride him.

The thirty-six runners included the previous year's winner

Grakle, running in the National for the sixth and last time, carrying 12 st 3lbs and ridden by Jack Fawcus. Joint-favourite with him was an Irish mare called Heartbreak Hill. Gregalach, the winner in 1929 and gallant runner-up to his former stable companion Grakle in 1931, was also in the field, ridden by the leading amateur Fred Thackeray.

Heartbreak Hill was going well when she was baulked by the huge riderless Pelorous Jack. Jack O'Grady pulled her out of a wing and took her back for another try, but she had lost too much ground to challenge effectively again. Grakle was baulked and Gregalach fell so heavily that Thackeray was unconscious for a fortnight and never rode in public again. Forbra and Egremont, ridden by Edward Paget, a London stockbroker who was later to have horses with Peter Cazalet, were both carrying 10 st 7 lb. They came together at the start of the final circuit and jumped ten fences neck and neck. As they came to the last upsides there was only one danger to them, Annandale. But Forbra and Egremont jumped the fence well and Annandale fell. On that long run-in which has seen the defeat of so many good horses carrying heavy weights Forbra's flat-race breeding came to his rescue and he won by three lengths. The 1930 winner Shaun Goilin, despite his weight of 12 st 4 lb, finished third. Heartbreak Hill finished the course in sixth place. It was a tremendous triumph for my father and for Kinnersley, which was, however, no stranger to National winners. In 1862 and 1863 Lord Coventry had sent out Emblem and his sister Emblematic to win the great chase from his yard only a mile and a half away.

Forbra was a great Liverpool horse. Although from now on he had just a little too much weight, he ran twice more in the National finishing sixth and fourth. He never made a mistake there. The only time that I rode him was in his last race when he split a pastern at Newbury and had to be put down.

I was already no stranger to death. While I was still an apprentice at the age of sixteen, my father had bought me a splendid hunter called Peter. At dusk one evening hounds were still running when we fell into a big brook on the Maddersfield Estate. We were both stuck in the brook. It was freezing cold and I found that I could not get Peter out. Looking for the reason, I discovered that he had broken his hock. I sent a message to the gamekeeper to bring a gun. It was a terrible wait because the horse kept fighting and I had to hold his head up until the keeper eventually arrived. Even then, he, a grown man with so much experience of shooting and guns, refused to shoot the horse. So it was left to me aged sixteen to shoot my own beloved hunter.

Shortly after Forbra's National Billy Stott ended his fifth and final season as champion jockey. His title was taken for the next six years by Gerry Wilson who was to become my best friend and later my brother-in-law. The son of a horse dealer, he graduated from minor meetings and would always say with a grin: 'I get paid for what I like doing best.' He was a wonderful horseman, tough and fearless. Whenever the going is like a bog and the stewards are talking of abandoning a meeting I am apt to say: 'Gerry would have called this good jumping ground!' For some reason this remark always seems to annoy a few people today. His horsemanship came from a lifetime spent in the hunting field and he taught me so much. I modelled myself on him, particularly through a race when he had no equal. I believe that he and old Jack Moloney had the best hands of any jockey I have ever known. Gerry was a wonderful jockey and the kindest of men. But he was also the toughest. There was no quarter after he left the weighing room. He was so determined and had such an intense will to win that he never gave up.

Once I started riding over fences I was prepared to get up on anything. I rode a horse called Provocative in the Grand National and was offered £100 for the ride and an extra £100 if he finished. He was lame going to the post and Perry Harding, the top class amateur who won the Champion Hurdle and later became a General, said to me at the start: 'That old horse of yours isn't quite right.' I said I knew he appeared lame but that I had to have a go. Perry replied: 'You've no need to ride him.' I told him that I had to because Jack Anthony who trained the horse had had a big bet that Provocative would complete the course. I wanted the money for the ride. Perry said: 'Well, if I were you, I'd settle for the first hundred, let him come under starter's orders and pull him up after he's jumped the first fence.'

Provocative jumped the first fence but then I found that I could not pull him up. By the time we had got to the second he had warmed up and he jumped all the way round the full four and a half miles. He finished up lame, but all the connections were delighted because of their bet that he would complete the course. In those days they used to bet 6 to 1 against any horse completing the course. The fences were bigger, straighter and nothing like as inviting as they are today. The water was sixteen foot.

The jumping game altogether is so very different from the flat, which that brave jockey Jack Dowdeswell once described as 'just going down and coming back'. First the journey to and from the meeting, frequently affected by the many hazards of an English winter: the snow, ice, fog and flooding, is frequently an adventure in itself. I think that most experienced jump trainers and jockeys would make outstanding rally drivers over any course and in any conditions. Then there is the race. One of the truest sayings is that there is a story in every National Hunt race. Apart from the thrills and the spills, the tireless, selfless St John's Ambulance men and the ambulances, human and equine, which are an integral part of the National Hunt scene, the horses race much longer and become better known than their flat counterparts. There is the young horse that gallops and jumps with the fire and promise of a future champion. There is the horse that is bought in the rough out of a field for a song by a small country grocer. And there is the animal, like my good horse Zarib, who breaks down and returns after an enforced lay-off of two years to win good races. And there are the crowds of dedicated enthusiasts all over these islands who will brave the worst weather conditions and love to tramp out into the middle of the course to watch by a fence. They know their sport and they love it.

In those days when I first started riding over obstacles there was also a kind of rough justice and, provided that they knew that the right spirit was there, officials who lived their lives on the racecourse were sometimes inclined to turn a blind eye. For example we all knew that the horse which appeared with boots or bandages all round, fore and aft, was not trying—'not off'. And, although jockeys were then, as now, strictly forbidden on principle to bet, it was sometimes better to safeguard yourself by letting it be known that one of your close associates had a financial interest in your mount winning.

When Gerry Wilson was courting my sister Vera, he was, as

the great champion jockey, often asked to ride more than one horse in a race and, in order to keep in with our family, he would sometimes put the lad whom he hoped to make his brother-in-law in for a few spare rides. That was how I came to ride for a splendid old Yorkshireman called Tommy of Tadcaster. He used to telephone and say; 'This is Tommy of Tadcaster. You comin' t' Haydock, aye? Then ride old Coleraine.' He was a great character, a fair trainer and a good friend. One day when I was up there riding for him, a man came up and asked: 'Will you ride my horse in the seller?' I, of course, said yes. I would ride anything. Then he said: 'I want you to stop him for me.'

I said nothing more but, as I set off for the weighing room, I found that old Tommy has been watching us. He said in that broad Yorkshire dialect: 'Did that chap ask you to ride old horse for him lad?' I nodded.

Tommy said: 'For Pete's sake be careful. He's been stopping him all the year and if you're not careful they'll have you straight in front of the stewards. You'd better have a pony on 'im with me.' I said that sounded all right.

I carried on to the weighing room and was starting to change when Gerry, who was riding a well-fancied horse called Ferrule in the same race, came up and asked: 'Are you riding that old horse then?'

'Yes,' I said.

'He doesn't fancy him you know.'

'I know hc doesn't.'

'Well you'd better have a pony on mine.'

'No,' I said. 'I have a pony on my own.'

I do not think that Gerry really believed me. But in the race my horse, who like most old selling chasers jumped as second nature, ran a bit free and I let him gallop on in front. I made no attempt to restrain him and he won. I rode in to the usual applause but I could see that my owner-trainer was livid. And, as I unsaddled, he said: 'I told all my book-maker pals to lay against this one.'

I said: 'Bad luck. I couldn't stop him anyway!'

I think the same man was warned off over some other offence not very long afterwards. Gerry, who had been trying for his life on Ferrule, the horse that they had all gone for, was furious. But it never lasted long and we were having a drink together before the end of the day.

In 1934 and 1935 Gerry was involved in one of the biggest sensations of the turf as the rider of the horse, hailed as the greatest steeplechaser of all times. Although I was only twenty-one at the time, I would, as the man nearest to him for the remainder of his life, like to take this opportunity of putting the records straight once and for all.

Golden Miller, sired by the moderate stallion Gold Court, was bred in Ireland by Lawrence Geraghty on a farm in County Meath. A huge golden chestnut with big bones, he was sold as a yearling at Dublin sales for 100 guineas. No one thought anything of him until Basil Briscoe, who trained in Cambridgeshire, brought him to England and ran him as a three-year-old over hurdles at Southwell. With that huge frame and mighty power, he was obviously destined for steeplechasing and, after being narrowly beaten at Newbury, he was bought by Philip Carr, father of the Nottinghamshire cricketer A. W. Carr, for £1,000. On Carr's death shortly afterwards, this magnificent power-packed racehorse, whose like we never see nowadays, was bought for £600 by the late Charlie Rogers for Dorothy Paget, the fabulous patron of National Hunt racing who became a legend in her own lifetime through her dress—that famous everlasting old grey coat—and her constant entourage of secretaries, her immense appetite, her habit of living at night and her rudeness which probably stemmed from shyness. She would lock herself in the lavatory at a race meeting until all the people had left. Then Lord Queenborough's daughter would emerge to eat a dinner as large as those Henry VIII enjoyed, firing questions at her trainer and her attendants.

By the end of March 1934 Gerry Wilson the champion jockey had had more than his share of falls, but he was in no way deterred and was riding stronger and better than ever. Golden Miller, for whom Basil Briscoe booked Gerry in the National, had only one fall to blemish his record and that at the Canal the previous year where, as a six-year-old, he had run understandably green over the big Liverpool fences. He had now won three Cheltenham Gold Cups—more then than any horse in the history of the jumping classic—and was attempting a unique double, the Gold Cup and the Grand National in the same year. Press, pundits and public alike were agreed that, if he achieved this feat, he would indeed be established as the horse of the century.

Now Aintree is a law unto itself. Walk round and you will be terrified by the size of the obstacles and amazed by the way that so many of them are set at what looks like an impossible angle. But when you are riding the course you meet those fences just right. On the other hand it is unique in that it has big drop fences like Becher's Brook where the landing is much lower than the take-off. Golden Miller, standing over 17 hands, with a huge heavy powerful shoulder, was inclined to jump off his forehand, and many experts doubted whether he was physically capable of jumping the big drops without making a mistake or falling. Moreover, although if he appeared in the paddock at Cheltenham today he would seem like a carthorse compared with some of our modern chasers, he had a fair bit of quality and was considered to be lacking in the ruggedness then demanded of an Aintree horse. This type had become traditional because the Irish used to put thoroughbreds to draught mares, thereby producing a big tough type of animal much coveted by the late Lord Bicester who used to insist that a chaser should 'walk away looking as though he had just shat himself.'

Basil Briscoe had produced the 8 to 1 favourite in perfect shape. There were several dangers, including our Forbra, Gregalach and Thomond II, owned by Dorothy Paget's popular American cousin Jock Whitney, who had had his disappointments at Liverpool with brilliant Easter Hero. Thomond II was tiny compared with the mighty Miller and was frequently described as two planks strapped together or 'the ham sandwich', because he was so narrow; but he was a great jumper and an out-and-out stayer. On this occasion the Miller had 12 st 2 lb, the same weight that he had carried the previous year, and Thomond II was set to carry two pounds less. Gerry rode a copy-book race. At the last fence he was a length behind Delaneige with Forbra and Thomond II in challenging positions. But Golden Miller proved his class by coming impressively up the run-in to win by five lengths from Delaneige with Thomond II third and Forbra fourth. The time was eight seconds faster than the record set up the year before by Kellsboro' Jack despite the fact that the Miller was carrying 7 lb more weight. Gerry and his great horse had achieved that remarkable double; they were considered unbeatable in their bid to achieve the same feat a year later.

Before Cheltenham the wonder horse was already down to 2 to 1 for the 1935 National. And for the Gold Cup he was unbackable, particularly since his only possible rival Thomond II was regarded as a non-runner. A few evenings before the National Hunt Festival Meeting Gerry had, as so often before and since, to tread the jumping jockeys' familiar path to an orthopaedic surgeon in London. Leaving the consulting room he went out into the cool March night air and walked up Harley Street until he found a newspaper boy. As he opened his paper under a street lamp, he forgot the racing results.

'The first thing I read,' he told me, 'was an announcement that, after all Jack Anthony had decided to run Thomond II. Jack, who had ridden three National winners, was a shrewd man and a good trainer. He wouldn't advise Mr Whitney to run if he did not think he had a real good chance of winning the Gold Cup. So I braced myself for a hard struggle and that's how it turned out, the greatest race of my life.'

When young Basil Briscoe was told the news he said: 'That's put the cat amongst the pigeons!'

Nevertheless the record crowd at Cheltenham on that fine overcast day backed Golden Miller down to odds on in the five horse field on perfect fast ground. Our local hero Billy Speck, one of the best jockeys never to win the championship, had the mount on Thomond II and from the start the two rivals dominated the race. Flying the fences at a record-shattering break-neck pace, neither jockey gave an inch. Down the hill Specky seized the rails so that Gerry had to come round the final bend into the straight on the outside.

Later Gerry decribed that never-to-be-forgotten finish to me.

'We fought it out neck and neck,' he said. 'There was never an inch between us as we headed for the last fence. We took off together and the two horses didn't jump it as you and I know jumping. They flew over it and flew the distance of the run-in too. It's a short run-in from the last to the winning post at Cheltenham, as you know only too well—no more than 240 yards —but it is a tiring uphill climb and any horse the least bit short of stamina falls back beaten as so many do year after year. Both Golden Miller and Thomond were thorough stayers and Specky as well as myself could ride a strong finish. But my horse found rather the better speed and we won all-out by three quarters of a length.'

In fact it was the strength and superb horsemanship of Gerry, the only man ever to remain champion jump jockey for six successive seasons, that won that epic struggle for Dorothy Paget who had been furiously hitting Charlie Rogers as the two horses battled together 'Why didn't you buy me the other horse too, Romeo?' She always called the large tall Irishman Romeo for some strange reason best known to herself.

In the previous year's National the Miller, ridden by the same jockey with two lbs more, had beaten Thomond II by ten lengths. Both were booked for Liverpool again and the pundits believed that desperate duel would take its toll on little Thomond II. As so often happens, they were wrong. The wiry tough 'ham sandwich' finished third again—this time to Reynoldstown—but, although his rival continued racing to win one more Gold Cup, his days as an effective force were numbered.

I don't think that I have ever seen a better race either flat or jumping. Perhaps it was the speed and the way that the two horses flew their obstacles that gave that tremendous thrill. The winner's record time for Cheltenham's very stiff Gold Cup course of three and a quarter undulating miles worked out at more than thirty-one miles per hour, or only about five miles an hour slower than a high class flat miler. You needed no horse knowledge and only a little common sense to realise that after that stupendous battle something had to give.

In fact I am certain that the Miller's disastrous return to Liverpool as raging hot favourite, which will always be accounted one of the mysteries of the turf, was most probably the result of that bitter struggle at Cheltenham. As far as I am concerned there was no mystery at all about the débâcle at the fence after Valentine's first time round. Although it was forty-two years ago, I talked with Gerry about it on a number of occasions and I remember it as though it were yesterday.

Golden Miller was carrying top weight of 12 st 7 lb. Nevertheless he was favourite at the ridiculous odds of 2 to 1, the shortest price since the odds on Mathew in 1847. In the paddock he dwarfed his twenty-six rivals and everyone considered that the National was a foregone conclusion—a case of 'Golden Miller first and the rest nowhere' as they had said once many years earlier of another mighty chestnut, Eclipse. But this time their faith was not to be justified. Golden Miller jumped the early fences brilliantly, but coming to Valentine's Brook for the first time, he seemed to be propping, shortening his stride as though he wanted to refuse. Gerry wouldn't let him. With all his tremendous strength he sat down and drove Golden Miller into that fence, forcing the big horse, who had already got too close for a perfect jump, to take off, lifting him over the obstacle. The favourite screwed appallingly in his take-off and pitched heavily on landing giving even Gerry no possible chance of staying on board. There was no doubt that a lot of people tried to say that Gerry threw himself off but that was plain rubbish. Gerry told me simply: 'The horse tried to refuse and pitched badly on landing shooting me over his head.'

I have since talked to many other eye witnesses. Fulke Walwyn, who was to ride that year's winner, Reynoldstown, to a second victory the following year, said: 'Gerry had no chance. No jockey could have stayed on when Golden Miller first tried to stop and then screwed over the fence landing awkwardly.' Ryan Price said: 'He jumped sideways and pitched. Even Gerry couldn't stay on board.' But the mystery and widespread malicious allegations of foul play caused Miss Paget to break with Gerry and with Basil Briscoe. There were two main reasons. The first was that the favourite, Jack Jarvis's Flamenco, had won the Lincoln at 8 to 1. Golden Miller was the second leg of a spring double involving an all-time record pay-out that would have ruined many of the bookies. Secondly no member of the racing press saw the incident for some strange reason. So that the first time the scribes knew that Golden Miller was no longer among the runners still standing was when the field approached the water jump at half way.

The Grand National in those days was run on a Friday. After the race vets examined Golden Miller and passed him sound, none the worse for his efforts. So Dorothy Paget decided that her champion, who had had an awful lot of racing that season, should take his chance again the following day in the Champion Chase over the Liverpool fences. At first they asked me to ride him but then changed their minds and decided to put Gerry up again. Golden Miller had no heart for racing at Liverpool. He reached the first fence and half-jumped, once again unseating the unfortunate Gerry. The angry howl of booing which greeted this fresh disaster was not for the jockey but for those who went to the well too often, asking a good horse to give more than he was capable of. Instead of the lavish celebration party at Liverpool's Adelphi Hotel the previous year Dorothy Paget immediately removed Golden Miller and her other horses from Basil Briscoe and sent them first to Donald Snow and later to Owen Anthony. Poor Basil moved to Royston, where he trained Commander III to win the Cambridgeshire. But he never got going again, soon gave up his licence, peddled dung and finally died a broken man in 1951.

Later in life I was to realise what was surely now only too obvious: that a top horse remains at his real peak for no more than three seasons. This is particularly so when he has had a lot of hard races and that one at Cheltenham must have taken much more out of Golden Miller than anyone could possibly imagine. Trainers would do well to remember that, in conjunction with close races, long distance travelling—e.g. from Cambridgeshire to Cheltenham and back and from Cambridgeshire to Liverpool—saps a horse's energy much more than they think.

When dealing with that class of horse and race. I have come to agree with Vincent O'Brien, who says: 'A horse has a certain mileage. The problem is discovering when he is coming to the end.' Golden Miller was finally irreparably strained by that race at Cheltenham and from that day he was steadily deteriorating.

Next year Golden Miller won his fifth and last Gold Cup. But, although he was clearly a spent force Dorothy Paget typically flouted public opinion and ordered her trainer Owen Anthony to try again for the great double. This time Golden Miller's jockey was Evan Williams. I was an eye-witness of the disaster. In fact my mount Avenger shared favouritism with Golden Miller. Reynoldstown, now carrying 12 st 2lb had a different rider because Frank Furlong was worried by increasing weight and had offered the ride to Fulke Walwyn, then an amateur, who had served with him in the 9th Lancers. In fact it was one of those amateur years. Davy Jones, a tubed cast-off from the flat, was ridden by Anthony Mildmay, later to become Lord Mildmay, one of the most popular riders and supporters of steeplechasing of all time, and Ego, whose dam had been exchanged in Ireland for a box of eggs, was ridden by his owner Harry Llewellyn, later to earn fame as an Olympic gold medallist with Foxhunter in the showjumping field.

Avenger, who was trained by my father for our eighty-year-old owner Mrs Violet Mundy, was a hell of a horse. He was a really handsome slashing all-quality animal who would have won any long-distance flat race. Specky used to ride him in the early days and he always used to jump the water badly. In the end, however, we managed to get him jumping the water quite well. The latest of his victories was in the National Hunt Handicap Chase at Cheltenham, so he was a worthy favourite. Golden Miller, despite all the scandal and public quarrels, and the well-held belief that he hated Aintree, was backed out of loyalty. He was a public hero. And not until Arkle would there be another horse like him.

As we jumped off and started that long gallop over the Melling Road to the first fence, I saw that Golden Miller's ears were back and his tail was swishing. He was obviously hating this return to Liverpool. Sure enough as we jumped the first fence I saw the blue and yellow colours of Dorothy Paget fall. I galloped on, happy that that potential danger was out of the way. Avenger was going beautifully and at the big open ditch called the Chair that's in front of the stands, we were lying second to Mildmay on Davy Jones. But once again the water, that huge water jump that has since been reduced, was Avenger's undoing. He dropped his hind legs in it and probably ricked his back. Whatever the reason, he had lost his freedom of action and impetus when we came to the next fence, the one that had been the first after the start. There he fell, breaking his neck and shattering the hopes of Mrs Mundy who had been trying for forty years to win that race. As I picked myself up cursing, I had a good view of the rest of the race. Evan Williams had held on to Golden Miller and had remounted but, already far behind after his fall, he had jumped only until the ditch after Valentine's. There Golden Miller refused and, despite repeated attempts, steadfastly confirmed that he hated Aintree.

Davey Jones, still in a commanding lead although making a

noise like a steam engine jumped the second last well but pecked slightly on landing and Anthony Mildmay paid the penalty for failing to tie a knot in his reins before the start. He slipped them correctly but the prong of the buckle slipped through the hasp. He lost control and with it the chance of achieving his greatest ambition. Reynoldstown was left in front with nothing to beat except Ego who finished twelve lengths behind. It is silly to say that he was lucky to join that rare band of dual National winners. His rival lost because of a mistake and you cannot afford to make mistakes if you want to win the best prizes.

Next year Dorothy Paget, a glutton for the punishment of her horse, put Danny Morgan on Golden Miller, but once again the chestnut refused at the ditch after Valentine's. Mercifully that was his last attempt. Evan Williams, the unfortunate rider in 1936, was now compensated when he won on Royal Mail.

I had a brief but stormy session riding for Dorothy Paget. Owen Anthony booked me to ride Aldene in the Liverpool Hurdle. Although he was a really useful performer on the flat, he had been busy all the season over hurdles. When I went into the paddock Owen passed on the owner's order. 'Win a short head, or get beat a short head,' he said. I managed neither but only succeeded in finishing third. When I returned there was hell to pay. I was supposed to ride Atco for Miss Paget in the steeplechase but after that rocket I went into the weighing room and threw my saddle down on the table saying I was damned if I would ride it.

Owen came in and said: 'Miss Paget is very upset. She's sorry for what she said and will you still ride the horse?'

So I went out into the paddock, where she told me: 'I want you to jump this horse off in front and make all the running.' He was only a novice and I knew that he didn't really get the trip. So I did not jump him off but just settled him down sensibly and let him jump to the front after the last ditch before I came on to the racecourse. I jumped the second last six lengths in front but the horse still did not stay and I was beaten two lengths by one of Lord Bicester's ridden by Tommy Carey. So I got the sack from old Dorothy and didn't ride for her again for a long time after that.

When I started to ride for her once more, I was booked for a horse called Speckled Band at Windsor. Her chief secretary Ruth Charlton, who subsequently married Charlie Smirke, was in the paddock and told me; 'I have a three-page letter for you from Miss Paget telling you how to ride the horse. Shall I read to it you?'

I said: 'Don't bother, Ruth.' And it got beaten. It wouldn't have won whatever the orders!

VI Partnership

My life took on an entirely new meaning in the summer of 1936. At a tennis party with friends on the other side of Worcestershire I met Mercy. Love at first sight is perhaps a slightly stupid expression but there is no doubt that in our case it was love at the first meeting. Mercy looked sensational—as she has done ever since. Dark-haired and slim, with a lovely complexion and a beautiful figure, she was perfectly turned out. We were both young, supremely fit and full of fun. We played tennis, drank, laughed and joked, but our eyes kept coming back to each other. Although we had never met before we were not strangers. Mercy knew that I was now one of the leading jump jockeys and I'd heard of her prowess in the hunting field and in point-to-points. I knew that she had represented England in France at the age of ten, that starting on a horse called Leicester Square at Banner Hill, the North Warwickshire Hunt meeting, when she was only fourteen, she had ridden numerous point-to-point winners; and that, despite her tender years Mercy Cockburn had no superior in the hunting field over those huge Warwickshire fences. We talked about each other and about horses. We made arrangements to meet again. And by the time we parted that evening we already knew in our hearts that we were made for each other.

Apart from her local meetings, Warwick and Stratford, Mercy had not been to races often before we met. Her interests were mainly confined to hunting, point-to-pointing and showing. But now, as soon as the new season started, she accompanied me to the races and life took on a new dimension. Highly intelligent, with a good eye for a horse, Mercy quickly absorbed the atmosphere and learnt everything about the sport.

Whenever we could we would still snatch a day's hunting either in Mercy's country or at home with the Croome where, of course, I would mount my fiancée, as she soon became, on my best hunter. I had a very good hunter in those days, the same fellow who had ducked me in Bow Brook in the first chapter. I liked to think that he had improved since then! Anyway Mercy, looking a picture as always, rode him sidesaddle one particular day when Gerry Wilson and I were free to hunt because there was no racing. Gerry was always a devil to go, who would take on anything and anyone. Like the Irish, he was always determined to win the hunt. But Mercy had a secret ambition. She had determined to jump Bow Brook. Her chance came sooner than she expected. Hounds were running hard and there in front of her loomed the brook. She galloped on fearlessly, gave her horse the office at just the right time and sailed over it. Gerry, the champion jockey, following just behind, had no intention of having his eye wiped by a girl. He drove on to the brook, his horse jumped and Gerry hit a branch, knocking out his teeth. As someone else came along behind, there was the champion, still hanging from the branch. He lost all his teeth that day in Bow Brook!

I thought I had a bit of a chance in the National of 1937, which, as I said earlier, was won by Royal Mail. I'd been booked to ride Delaneige, who had started challenging at Aintree back in 1933, when Kellsboro' Jack had won for the American Mrs Ambrose Clark. That year Delaneige was fourth. In 1934 he was the runner-up, beaten five lengths by Golden Miller. Although he had fallen in 1936, I knew that I had a sound Aintree mount. Unfortunately we became involved in one of those all-too-frequent Liverpool mix-ups and I was clouted out of the saddle.

We married just forty years ago on 23rd June 1937. After our honeymoon, we settled near Kinnersley at Church Farm, Severn Stoke where we had a small yard as well as a nice house. Now we were able to go racing together all the time. Ever since, we have shared everything, all our joys, all our disappointments, all our secrets. I am sure that this is why so many trainers' and farmers' marriages are successful. The very nature of your job makes you dependent on each other. When a trainer has runners at two meetings, he will go to one and his wife to the other. When they return home, they exchange experiences and tell each other how the various animals ran. The wife of a trainer has a full time job. Apart from looking after any children, she can fulfil herself by looking after the staff and their families, entertaining the owners, and, in Mercy's case, taking charge of the administrative side of the business. Now, however, newly married, we were able to enjoy each other's company and share the driving to the various race meetings.

To introduce the girl I was marrying, let me ask Mercy to describe one of the most fascinating episodes of her childhood.

'When I was ten years old a very well known artist called Cecil Aldin, whose hunting, racing and dog pictures can be found all over the country, took eight child riders to France to represent England.

'We were taken to Le Touquet where we were all entertained at the Hermitage Hotel and had a fabulous time. I had a top-class pony called The Sheikh, who had won at the best shows all over England, including The Royal. I rode him representing his height of 12 hands 2 inches, which was obviously ideal for my age group. The pony won and I was presented with my trophy by the Prince of Wales, later King Edward VIII, who was at Le Touquet with Mrs Dudley Ward.

'Our success did not go unnoticed. One of the Princess Hohenlohe of Landenberg's agents saw my pony and decided that it should be bought for her five children of whom the eldest was Penelope and the second Prince Alfonso.

'So they sent a representative over to our home in Warwickshire to inspect the pony. He bought it and took it back to Spain for the children to ride.

'Now, when the Sheikh had been there for about six months, Princess Hohenlohe wrote to my mother asking if I would go out to ride the pony because they did not think that they had got it going properly. In those days before the Civil War, it was quite a major step to travel to Spain by train (there were virtually no aeroplanes to Spain in those days) for a child of eleven accompanied by a mother who did not speak a word of either French or Spanish. Furthermore we suffered under the misguided impression that Spain had telephones and post offices just like those in England. This was not so.

'We caught the express from Calais and went down over the Pyrenees to Escorial, which was, we understood, close to the home of our hosts. (Recently, the Queen, whose horses are always so cleverly named, had a good classic filly by Royal Palace out of Asturia, which she called Escorial and with which she won the Musidora Stakes.) Little did we know that distance means nothing in Spain and that the vast château for which we were bound was some forty miles over the mountains from Escorial, which in turn was about two hundred miles from Madrid. We had sent a cable and so assumed that we would be met. But this was not England. The nearest post office was forty miles away and telephones hardly worked at all.

'My mother and I arrived at Escorial station late at night and tried to explain to the depleted staff where we wanted to go. It was dark, and as my mother did not speak a word of Spanish, this was no easy task, particularly as the letter which we showed from our host was on headed writing paper and, as the Civil War was about to erupt the following year, Royalty was not particularly popular.

'Eventually there appeared a man who could have stepped straight out of a gangster film. He had only one arm, wore a black patch over one eye, a black beret and a long black leather coat. There was no sign of a smile beneath his thin black moustache as he motioned us to get into a large black motor car. There was nothing for it. My mother and I got in and were driven for what seemed like hours round terrifying hair-pin bends over the mountains, never seeing a light for forty miles. The further we went the more frightened my mother became and it was lucky that I was too young to realise all the possible implications. Suddenly we arrived at some enormous gates resembling the portcullis of a medieval castle, which was, as it turned out, just about what we were approaching. Our driver blew his horn and the vast gates opened. My mother said: "This is definitely an RC Convent. We will never be seen again!"

'However our troubles ended when we were ushered into the castle where we were welcomed with opened arms. Our hosts were full of apologies because they had not received our cable and thought we were coming two weeks later. All was well and the hospitality was fantastic. It was a remarkable taste of wonderful old-world hospitality. We stayed for a fortnight during which I rode the pony most of the time and taught the children including

Prince Alfonso to get on better with him. It was truly a memorable visit.'

Many years later Mercy and I were staying on the Costa del Sol at the Marbella Club. One day when we were playing tennis I ricked my ankle and decided that this would be a good excuse to go into the bar, where I met the man who runs this famous club and whom I recognised immediately from all the photographs as Prince Alfonso, the King of Spain's nephew, who had married Princess Ira when she was fifteen years old.

I said: 'I think you knew my wife many years ago.'

Alfonso asked: 'What was her name?'

'Mercy—Mercy Cockburn.'

He never hesitated. 'Of course!' he said. 'Of course I remember her well. She was the first little girl I ever saw in jodhpurs.'

From that moment on we never looked back. He gave us a fantastic evening and the following day found us some aeroplane seats to fly to Tangier, booked our hotel rooms there and was generosity itself. For the umpteenth time I appreciated my good fortune in marrying Mercy.

It was in the late '50s when we had another experience of Spanish hospitality and of the feudalism that still exists in that country.

Eight English horses were invited by the Spanish Jockey Club to run in Madrid. Ryan Price sent two; Ivor Herbert, Ken Bailey, Dave Hanley and someone else sent one each. The races were all amateur events and so our English party included John Lawrence (later Oaksey) and his future wife Tory. Our large son Guy (all 6 feet 4 inches of him) travelled as a lad, looking after the horses.

We took off from Southend in an unpressurised old Dakota carrying the eight horses. In addition to Mercy, the girls included Ivor's first wife Jenny Herbert and Ken's wife Biddy Bailey. There was no lavatory on board and, owing to the lack of pressurisation, it was abominably cold and the journey seemed to take hours and hours. There was considerable relief when we eventually came down to Bordeaux to refuel. There, once on the tarmac we found that it was swelteringly hot. I wanted to open the front of the aeroplane in order to let the horses have some air and to give them some water. But the pilot refused point blank. However, finally he and his navigator left the aircraft to get some refreshment and I immediately opened up the front. There was all hell to pay when they got back and the pilot threatened not to take off. I didn't care. The horses had had their air and had enjoyed their water. Needless to say we took off all right.

Dave, Guy, Ivor and I played cards all the way sitting on a bale of hay. As we couldn't hear ourselves speak, we played pontoon by signs. The noise was appalling.

When we landed in Madrid, we found that the Spaniards had sent a large cattle truck to collect our horses. There were no partitions and, although I say it myself, it was a good thing that I, with my knowledge of the rough and ready as well as the best, was in the party. Ivor ran round in ever-decreasing circles like a bewildered hen that had lost its head, and refused to travel with the horses. So it was left to Guy and me. I tied them up in herring-bone fashion, head to tail all the way down the vehicle. Fortunately I also remembered to tie them with slip knots.

The driver was a demon. He set off at an enormous pace, which he kept up the whole way from the airport to the racecourse stables. Inevitably on the way one of the horses—it was Ivor's ironically—fell over. I had to climb over five horses to get to him, pulled the slip knot and all was well. Eventually we arrived safely at the stables.

The Spaniards laid on all sorts of wonderful entertainments. They had cocktail parties, dinners, lunches, receptions and so on. The *pièce de résistance* was the ball given by the Duke of Albuquerque. Still riding now at the age of fifty-nine, this splendid fellow is the most experienced amateur in Europe and probably in the world. He has ridden successfully in nine different countries and says: 'In England and Ireland I have found the best steeplechases.' He loves riding round Aintree and it was there that in 1976 he broke his leg on his horse Nereo. He has the nose and huge prominent chin of the traditional Spanish grandee which he undoubtedly is and it is said in Spain that that chin has ploughed more furrows in the turf than any other!

The entire English party had invitations to the ball at his home about twenty-five miles out of Madrid. We were taken out in a private bus and at the great entrance gates were halted by guards holding tommy-guns. When we were ushered in, the ball was the most fantastic party that Mercy and I have ever been to. Mercy says that never in her life has she seen such beautiful clothes and such fabulous jewellery. A number of the Spanish ladies had collars or chokers two inches in depth made of solid diamonds, sapphires or rubies. The obvious wealth was quite incredible.

There were four bands and all the staff were dressed in the Duke's own livery, green velvet jackets, knee breeches, white stockings and white gloves. Thirty of them marched in line into the great banqueting hall carrying silver platters with whole sucking pigs, sheep, beef, turkeys and every other kind of food that you can imagine. There were 600 guests and Albuquerque with his own staff staged the whole occasion with no outside help at all.

We did not win any races but one of our horses finished second. Anthony Porter was our jockey.

Altogether the whole trip was tremendous fun. Mercy and I were singled out to represent the British party at a bullfight, presumably because they thought that we were the least likely to be squeamish about it. It was a very high-class programme—a sort of top-of-the-first-division affair. We had VIP treatment. The ladies sat in one box and the men in another. We were refreshed with sherry and dry biscuits.

At the end of our stay we travelled back the same way that we had come—with the horses in that very ancient unpressurised Dakota which had to struggle desperately to get sufficient height to cross the Pyrenees. Some people went by more glamorous transport, but this suited us. Travelling with the horses on this freight plane, we went free!

The life of a jumping jockey's wife can be a worrying one. Some chaps are unluckier than others and always seem to be returning on stretchers to the ambulance room. Their poor wives have to wait to hear a doctor's verdict or follow the ambulance to the local hospital.

I was very lucky with falls. I broke my ankle once and my neck twice, but otherwise suffered nothing worse than concussion. On one such occasion after a bad fall I had been laid up for a few days and we had two or three good runners at Bangor-on-Dee. My father said: 'You're not fit, Fred. Let Gerry ride them.'

I was quietly furious but decided to go to the meeting anyway to see how the horses performed. My mother put us up a very nice picnic hamper and we went for the day out. Once again the best-laid plans went astray. Mellow from a good lunch I was enjoying watching Gerry go round in the first chase, when his mount never took off at the open ditch and turned a somersault, burying him. He was completely flattened. That was the end of his activities for the afternoon. I sprinted to the weighing room and had already pulled on my breeches when our owner, Sir Edward Hanmer, a steward of the meeting, came in. I said: 'I'm all right, sir. I'll be fit to ride.' My father followed disapprovingly, but I had already staked my claim and time was getting short. So I rode and won on the horse. Then I rode another animal in the novice chase, had a crashing fall and broke my ankle.*

My father trained for an old man called Lawson Walker who had a prefix for all his horses—Teme. For example Teme Star, Teme Willow, Teme Square and so on. In the end Wetherby's got into such a muddle with all these Temes that they became fed up and asked him to stop adding this prefix.

It was on Teme Willow that I won that ankle-breaking day at Bangor. Teme Square was a different cup of tea. He was a moderate sort of animal with a predilection for falling. In fact I think he fell six times in succession. One day we took him to Chepstow. Now with that undulating ground the first fence in the straight is invisible from the stands. Teme Square fell at the first in the straight. I caught him quickly, jumped up, got going again and was once more in touch with the leaders going down the hill turning into the straight for the second time. They say there are fools, damn fools and those who get up and go on again. Anyway bang! Down we came again at the same obstacle, the first in the straight out of sight of the stands. Once again I caught the old horse and climbed up. Just for a bit of practice I got onto the hurdle track and jumped the last two hurdles on the way home. When I came in old Lawson Walker was furious. 'What did you pull him up for? Why didn't you jump the last two fences?' he

*Today after an injury, a jockey must produce medical evidence on his official 'card' clearing him to ride again.

said. It took me some time to realise that he had not seen his horse fall again. The last time he had seen him, he was going nicely making up ground on the leaders.

I rode him again at Ludlow and won on him but then refused to ride him any more. I had done my stint. I had had five falls and had ridden him a winner, so I told my father: 'You can get who you like to ride him now!' Ginger Dennistoun came in for a lot of these rather dubious rides on the old horse.

I have so many happy memories of that wonderful racecourse Birmingham, dating back to my apprentice days on the flat. I was nearly caught out one day riding an unfancied runner in a race over that famous straight mile. The field split up at the start, the bulk racing on the far side of the course and only three, including me, on the near side. So I suppose that my efforts, or lack of them, were painfully obvious. Anyway I was called straight into the stewards' room. Now old Fred Withington, the only man ever to have held a professional trainer's licence and become a member of the ruling body of racing, was standing at the back of the stewards' room when I was marched in.

The senior steward looked at me over his spectacles. 'Rimell,' he said, 'why didn't you persevere on that horse? You merely flourished your whip for the benefit of the people on the stands!' I could see Fred Withington, a wonderful chap, putting his fingers in his mouth and tittering in his familiar way. I thought I was going to burst out laughing myself but I managed to keep a straight face and said: 'My Lord, gentlemen, the horse was hanging so badly that I couldn't let him down.' They had no patrol camera and only their memories to rely on. So they accepted my explanation. That was the second and the last time that I was ever up before the stewards on the flat.

My father bought a splendid horse called Knight of London for Mrs Mundy. The old man was a bit of a demon for schooling horses. He had a bee in his bonnet about it. We had schooled this horse over hurdles and he had won some good hurdle races. We had him in a decent novice chase at Birmingham and beforehand we schooled him at Cley Hill. He jumped perfectly, brilliantly.

About four days before Birmingham my father said: 'I think I'll just give that horse another jump.'

I said: 'He doesn't want it. He's perfectly all right.'

However, the old man was the boss and so off we went to school over our own fences. Knight of London had obviously had enough schooling as I surmised. He tried to stop going to the ditch and he slid into the guard rail, took the guard rail right through the fence into the field and turned head over heels. As I lay on the ground, I watched him gallop away, loose stirrups and reins flying. I got up and I was livid. I don't think I was ever as angry with my old man as I was that day.

So we set off for Birmingham. Down at the start I gave him a few nice cracks with my whip. I really worked him up to get over the effects of my father's excessive schooling and that fall. Up went the gate and he set off, round the turn on the far side, jumping the first and the ditch as though he had the devil on his tail. Then I settled him and rode a really nice race. After that he never looked back.

He was a very good horse indeed. I won the Cathcart Chase at Cheltenham on him. Gerry rode a very fancied horse in that race. I had had a terrible Cheltenham. I don't think that I had got over the last fence or last hurdle in any race during the three days and the Cathcart was the last race on the last day of the National Hunt meeting.

My father said: 'If everything were normal I think he'd win. Gerry says he'll win, so take him on. I reckon that Jim Newcombe, ridden by Tommy McNeill, is the one horse you have to beat. So take him on.'

As a result, from the moment the gate went up, I took them all on. I had beaten Jim Newcombe at the top of the hill and had about four in front of me coming down to the last fences when I looked round and saw that old Gerry was coming at me. I had to ride like a man possessed and just lasted home.

People talk an awful lot of rubbish these days about the high price of jumpers. In comparison with other things, the price is not high at all. At the time that we were married right up to the war you could buy a brand new Ford motor car for £100 and a packet of Player's cigarettes for just 11½d. You put a shilling in the slot machine and out came a packet with a halfpenny stuck in the cellophane wrapping. When my father went to Ireland to buy two top class horses at that time, he gave £4,500 for one and

The Hohenlohe children, including Prince Alfonso, 1929.

The Hohenlohe home.

Mercy Cockburn winning at the Birmingham Show, 1931.

Mercy out hunting with her mother.

Fred Rimell on Avenger leads Gerry Wilson on Custom House at Newbury.

Fred and Mercy Rimell, 1939.

Fred and Mercy take part in a parade of sport, 1950.

Scarlett Rimell and Peter Pan triumphant at the Windsor Show, 1950. *Below:* Princess Alice presents the trophy.

Mercy Rimell, *c.* 1958.

The Queen Mother's Devon Loch, ridden by Dick Francis (*right*), and the eventual winner, ESB ridden by Dave Dick, take the last fence during the 1956 Grand National. (*Sport & General*)

The winning Grand National combination: the owners, Leonard and Stella Carver, ESB, Dave Dick and Fred Rimell. (*Rex Colman: Baron*)

Scarlett Rimell on Nicolaus Silver.

£2,500 for the other. They were both first-class buys, Knight of London and Custom House, a splendid horse who won twenty-eight races. People who hunted on the top level in Leicestershire in those days reckoned to pay £500 each for their thoroughbred hunters to carry them with the Quorn, Cottesmore, Belvoir, etc. When you think of the extent to which everything else, including prize money, has risen since those days, it is surely ludicrous for people to complain about paying £10,000 and upwards for decent jumpers. Judged by the standards of yesteryear, they are expecting to get something for nothing. But the cost of production has risen fantastically. At the Houghton Sales in October 1976 throughout the catalogue the yearlings actually averaged more than 10,000 guineas.

If I was never to ride a Grand National winner myself, at least I was to be instrumental in winning one for a friend.

The big Aintree chase with its thrills and romance has always attracted the Americans, particularly the members of the rich foxhunting land-owning fraternity in the south like Mrs Scott, on whose land the famous international steeplechase, The Colonial Cup, is now run at Camden in South Carolina. But by 1938 thirty years had passed since the first American-bred winner Rubio had won for Major Douglas-Pennant. Subsequently American-owned Sergeant Murphy and Jack Horner succeeded and in 1933 Kellsboro' Jack won for Mrs Ambrose Clark. Billy Barton, Easter Hero and Thomond II had failed, but had got near enough to whet the appetite of transatlantic sportsmen. Now Mrs Scott herself challenged with what appeared to be a most unsuitable contestant, her eleven-year-old chestnut pony stallion, Battleship, who stood only 15 hands 2 inches. Her trainer was Reg Hobbs, that finest of horsemen who had nagged so successfully for the foxhunting Americans in Leicestershire. Reg, with the faith and confidence of one who has coached horse and rider together, entrusted Battleship to his seventeen-year-old son Bruce, who was already six feet tall.

I shall never forget riding in that parade as the thirty-six of us walked down in front of those huge stands at Liverpool. Tiny Battleship, a son of the classic American sire Man O' War, was wearing blinkers, a most unusual sight in the National. He was made to look even smaller not only by his tall, thin, youthfully handsome jockey, but also by all the other runners, including magnificent Irish Royal Danieli, who, ridden by popular Dan Moore, was strongly fancied. Not even the Americans could summon up enough confidence to support their representative with any conviction and he started at 40 to 1.

Dan had no fears about his mount. He took Royal Danieli to the front soon after the start and stayed there looking all over a winner. But at Becher's second time round we had just about joined him. I was upsides with Battleship as we approached the big drop fence, and although my chap was tiring, I could see that the American chestnut was going pretty well. But Battleship pecked as we landed well clear on the other side and Bruce was shot up his neck over his pony's ears with no hope of getting back into the plate. I stretched out a hand caught hold of him by the seat of his breeches and shouted: 'Where do you think you're going matey?' I dragged him back into the saddle and he galloped on. Me, I fell at the very next fence!

Even as I was rolling on the ground, Bruce was taking on Dan and now he had learned his lesson. When Battleship made his only other mistake three fences from home, he was ready for him, picked him up and kept him going. It was a tremendous battle from the last but David beat Goliath. The little horse was given the verdict by a head to the delight of the American contingent and the fury of the Irish.

That was Gerry's sixth consecutive championship season—a record which may never be broken. He was to win one more, but in the meantime I had other ideas. Throughout the 1938/9 season, which was the last to be completed for seven years, my brother-in-law and I were level-pegging just as Terry Biddlecombe and his brother-in-law Bob Davies were to be thirty years on. It was ding dong all the season. On the last day of racing we went to Newport, one of the little jumping meetings which has now sadly disappeared, with fifty-nine winners apiece. I rode a treble and Gerry had a blank day. So I was champion jockey for the first time and I had taken the title from the man I liked and admired most.

Our son Guy was born in November 1938. During the summer of 1939 Mercy and I were on top of the world.

But that little racing world of ours started to totter when war was declared in September 1939, although at first there seemed to be no cause for dismay.

I immediately joined up as an infantry soldier in the Bedfordshire and Hertfordshire Regiment. But they found out that I was medical category E and slung me out. So I managed to get taken on as an RAF driver at the big maintenance units in Worcestershire. For three years I was with 7MU at Quedgley and for two years with 25MU at Hartlebury. I drove those huge seventy foot 'Queen Marys', carrying all sorts of component parts sometimes to Glasgow, sometimes to the docks, sometimes over to Ireland. I tried to get away on Saturdays to ride at the restricted zoned race meetings. By this means I managed to retain my champion jockey's title, but with only twenty-four winners. Old Gerry, too badly knocked about to be considered for any war job, regained his title with twenty-two winners in 1940/41 and in 1941/2 Ron Smyth managed to get there with just twelve winners. The following two seasons there was no National Hunt racing at all, which I have always considered to have been an error of judgement. There was nothing better for morale for those who had loved the sport before the war than to come back on leave and enjoy the odd Saturday, or to read about it and follow it in the papers when they were absent on service.

Our daughter Scarlett was born in 1942. So Mercy was at home with two infants and virtually no money coming in at all. She had to earn some in the only way she knew—buying, breaking and selling ponies. For about twelve months she had some paying guests. She dealt entirely with ponies because we really had not the facilities for hunters and there was nobody to help at all, only her.

When the gymkhanas and horse shows got going again she attacked them with great zest. In those days we had no car because there was no petrol. She had a moped and a pony and trap and if she really wanted to go into Worcester or anywhere else, she would hitch-hike. In fact she hitched all over the place.

But these were dreary years for her as they were for other women all over the country left on their own with small children, struggling valiantly to make ends meet.

By 1943 when flat racing started to pick up again, albeit on a limited scale, my father had runners. He had no proper staff, no travelling head man, no box driver. There were no men about to do any of those jobs. So Mercy, with a couple of friends who worked on the farm, did the lot between them. The only means of getting to the meetings was in the horse box and so the easiest way was to drive it yourself, which she did. After the allied invasion of Europe the bastions of the Germans began to fall and the end of the war was in sight. So National Hunt racing struggled into life again. In the first season 1944/5 I shared the jockeys' championship with Frenchie Nicholson. We finished up with fifteen winners apiece.

Frenchie, an old friend and neighbour, put me through the wing at Cheltenham one day. He was suspended for the rest of the meeting.

Now Gerry had finally given up riding and was training. I rode for him as often as possible. One day at Windsor he booked me for an old tearaway horse called Right 'un. For obvious reasons this hard-pulling front-runner was not fancied to win. On that figure-of-eight course in particular, he used to jump right-handed at one fence and then left at another. He was jumping all over the racecourse with me, but I wasn't doing too much to stop him. Cliff Beechener first tried to come up on my inside and I went across him and when he went the other side I cut him off there. When we came in, he went to the stewards and accused me of foul riding. They fined him fifty pounds.

Cliff must have thought a bit about it because when I rode the old horse at Worcester, he took the trouble to go down the course and when he saw how Right 'un behaved, he went to the stewards and said that he wished to withdraw his accusation of foul riding that he had made at Windsor. So they fined him another fifty pounds!

The first time I broke my neck was at Wincanton. I had been riding Poet Prince. I was lying in the ambulance room when Mercy came in and said that I was booked for Wincanton Cottage Hospital. I said: 'Not on your nellie!'

So I sent the old medical attendant out to get some tea and, when he came back, I had gone. We got in the car and Mercy drove me back to Cheltenham stopping to telephone on the way there. It was a crazy thing to do, but in those days we didn't realise it. We were young, healthy and carefree. The doctor told me to go home and have a nice sleep and said that he would make arrangements for an X-ray in the morning. I could not sleep at all that night, I woke up in the morning to be as sick as a dog. Mercy took me into Cheltenham for the X-ray which discovered that I had broken my second vertebra. So they put me on some planks with sandbags which effectively prevented me from moving at all.

The most uncomfortable thing was the plaster cast which went right over my head and down to my waist. Just my face stuck out of it and Mercy says that I looked like some monster from a television horror programme.

I had to wear it for three months. It was the most uncomfortable time that I have even known. My beard started to grow and the only way that I could stop the irritation was by squirting powder up under the plaster. But that was soon not in the least effective. Finally I went to St Thomas's Hospital where Dr Perkins cut me out of the horrible cast. He said: 'I'll take you out of it if you promise me that you won't look round at the girls quickly for a week.'

So he cut it off and I remember walking back over London Bridge with my long hair and beard feeling horribly scruffy. All I wanted to do was to get to a barber for a hair cut, shave and shampoo. After that, and a hot bath, I felt a lot better.

On the second and last occasion that I broke my neck they put me in a lightweight collar which merely kept my head in position. That was a great deal better.

The race that gave me the greatest pleasure of my entire riding career was the 1945 Champion Hurdle which I won on Brains Trust. The reason for this was that the horse was trained by none other than Gerry Wilson.

Poor Flame was a very useful chaser my father had bought from James Hanbury and Tommy Nelson. We fancied him strongly to win the National Hunt Handicap Chase at Cheltenham.

But he jumped badly to the right on a left-handed course. Determined to make him jump straight, I hit him so hard that I lost my whip. I was desperate because he was dead lazy and I knew I ought to win, but how with no whip?

So when I saw Nicky Pinch on Black Hawk had no chance, I pulled upside shouting: 'You don't want that, do you?' and picked the whip out of his hand! Then I proceeded to ride a tremendous finish with my 'borrowed' whip. I don't think I have ever driven harder up that final hill and I got the verdict by a head. I had to give Nicky a fiver. We had a lot of fun in the weighing room in those days.

On one memorable day at Cheltenham I rode five winners in the afternoon and I managed the same feat at Windsor. In 1945/6, the first full season after the war, I was champion jockey again with fifty-four winners.

Gerry must have been one of the easiest trainers to ride for. He would give you fewer instructions than anybody that I ever knew. He'd come up in the paddock and say: 'This horse is very well. I think he'll win.' That's all. With another animal he might say: 'This horse has been laid up for a bit. Give him a bit of a chance.' No more.

One of the best horses I rode for him was Carnival Boy who won eight hurdle races on the trot and was a top-class performer although he never won the Champion Hurdle. In fact I always thought that he was a better horse than Brains Trust, who did. But perhaps he was not quite such a tough horse.

My brother-in-law played a nice little trick on me one day and caught me out properly. At the time he had two novice chasers one of whom, Radiance, was a decent horse, on whom I had already ridden a couple of winners, while the other was a great big camel of a chestnut called Jock belonging to Lord Roseberry. Bob Turnell rode Jock twice and twice he was buried properly. There were no overnight declarations in those days and Gerry had Radiance and Jock in the same race at Cheltenham. He told me beforehand: 'I'll run that Radiance and I'd like you to ride him.' Naturally I accepted. But when I got to the meeting and met Gerry, he said: 'I'm not running that horse Radiance after all. You'll ride Jock!' I called him every sort of bastard under the sun but I rode the horse and won by a length.

In the closing months of the war, when the result was at last a foregone conclusion, we had quite a lot of fun picking up the pieces and starting up again where we had left off. Fulke Walwyn's first wife Diana (formerly Di Carlos-Clarke) was a very lovely girl and a superb rider. She was like Marlene Dietrich on a horse. Everyone loved Di and she was tremendous value at a party. She and Fulke had started from nothing at Lambourn with broken down flat-race cast-offs, patched them up to win sellers and thus gradually built up a great reputation. There is no doubt in my mind that over the years Fulke is consistently the finest of all jumping trainers.

An interesting side line on Di, who was later to meet her end in particularly tragic circumstances, was that she was too vain to wear spectacles. She was also an extremely fast driver of big powerful cars. Which was all right until you realised how hopelessly short-sighted she was. Her language was of the saltiest and she was no respecter of persons. I was engaged by Di to ride her West Fell on the first day at Catterick, where I was due to ride Delightful Devon for Eric Ohlson on the second day of the meeting.

By now Mercy and I had acquired a large old Packard motor car. So the day before Di and Mercy and I set off for Richmond in Yorkshire to spend the night. It was freezing cold and in those days it was a monumental journey because there were no motorways and the roads were as bad or worse than they had been before the war. Of course we had no car heater and, by the time that we arrived at a horrible little hotel in Richmond, we were perished with cold.

As soon as we found our rooms, Di came down to the reception desk again and demanded a bath towel. She was met with the usual response, 'No towels. There's a war on!' Di flew off the handle and told the manager in no uncertain terms what she thought of him. Then she returned upstairs ran herself a large hot bath and soaked in it before drying herself on the counterpane.

In the grim little hotel lounge we found two dear old ladies knitting in front of an apology for a fire containing about three minute embers of coal. Di walked over, stood in front of the fire, lifted her skirt right up, leaving little to the imagination, and said loudly: 'God, it's fucking cold in here!'

The two old girls gathered up their knitting and rushed out of the room.

We made our own amusement because, of course, there was no television in those days. As the evening progressed we played a rather gruesome game called 'Coffee-Potting'. Someone goes out of the room and when he returns he has to try to guess what the others are thinking about. 'Do you Coffee-Pot above or below the navel?' 'Do you Coffee-Pot in bed?' and so on. That evening the game got very low indeed. One of George Owen's young amateurs was staying in the hotel and I do not believe that he had ever met any racing people before. He rode the next day and we never saw him again. He was so horrified at that sight of the racing world that he just vanished.

West Fell duly won on the first day but Sir Eric Ohlson never stopped telling me that his horse Delightful Devon was not fancied and had no chance. However by the time of the start on the second day I had made up my mind that he was going to win in any case and win he did.

I rode a number of winners for Fulke and he asked me to take over as his stable jockey. But I had just had the pleasure of helping Gerry to become champion trainer while I was champion jockey and I remained loyal to my old friend. At the beginning of the next season I went to Lambourn to see Fulke's yard and realised what a lovely string he had. After I'd been round Gerry's yard I knew that I had made a mistake but I could do nothing about it. That was the first year that Bryan Marshall rode for Fulke. In fact after I had had a fall I put Bryan in for the ride on Leap Man and he never looked back.

We had some wild parties and there was no better performer than Fulke, although latterly he got Dave Dick to fight his battles for him! One of our happy hunting grounds was the Imperial Hotel at Torquay during the Devon circuit at the little courses in the South West. One night we had a tremendous party with Fulke, a number of other jumping jockeys and trainers, bookmaker Fred Binns and some of his henchmen. We carried the piano downstairs into the bottom bar and with it a somewhat odd pianist. Every time he was not looking at the piano Fulke was pouring champagne into the back of the instrument. In the end the pianist had only about four notes to play. Next morning I returned from the racecourse to find the manager of the Imperial with the piano on the balcony taking the back off. I asked him what he was doing. He said: 'Somebody got the piano pissed last night and I'm trying to dry it out!'

VII *Training*

In those years immediately after the war I had to waste very hard. During the summer I would go up to 12 st and then, when the season started, I had to be down to about 10 st 6 lb. It was a tremendous effort, which grew harder as time went by. I have the highest possible respect and admiration for Lester Piggott who is so dedicated that he can keep his weight down all the year round. But then jumping jockeys have always enjoyed the 'eat, drink and be merry' philosophy and it is hard to keep your weight at exactly the same level.

I knew that the writing was on the wall and that I would soon have to give up riding and start training. If you can begin while you are in demand as a jockey, people send you horses just so that they can be ridden by you, so at the start of the 1946/7 season I took out a licence. In the beginning I had a few horses down in Severn Stoke. The first winner I trained was a horse called Tabora owned by Tom Hill the publican of the famous Chequers at Cutnall Green. I rode him myself to win a maiden hurdle at Cheltenham. Tom Hill was very friendly with a number of racing people including Reg Hobbs and also with the Oliver brothers, Worcestershire farmers and cattle dealers whom he brought into racing.

My father had always intended to hand Kinnersley over to me. So, when I started training down in the bottom yard at Church House and pinched a few of his owners, collecting about sixteen horses, he had already decided to move to Windsor House, Lambourn with his predominantly flat team and leave the way open to me in Worcestershire. I shall always be grateful to him. It was entirely his own idea and he was extremely successful at Lambourn, training such good horses as Damremont and Chivalry, with whom he won the Victoria Cup and the Royal Hunt Cup.

Coloured Schoolboy was easily the best horse I trained in those early years. Although he had started the season as a novice, I won six good races on him and by 12th April he was entitled to start as second favourite at 4 to 1 for the Cheltenham Gold Cup. The favourite was Dorothy Paget's Happy Home, ridden by Dan Moore. But Lord Grimthorpe had bought a six-year-old French chaser, a glamorous little all-quality golden chestnut who had won the Lancaster Chase at Manchester on his only outing in this country. Fortina, as he was called, was trained by that splendid sportsman the late Hector Christie and ridden by amateur Dicky Black.

The National Hunt meeting that year had been first postponed owing to frost and snow and then abandoned. The Gold Cup and the Champion Hurdle were carried forward to the April meeting. They were run on the Saturday. The second and third days were to be Monday and Tuesday. So the course was fresh and the going was good and fast.

We went a tremendous gallop, led initially by Chaka, ridden by Ron Smyth with Fabiano, a French trained candidate, Happy Home and Fortina close up.

At the ditch before the water down the back straight second time round Coloured Schoolboy was going very well but not quite well enough. I will always swear that somebody was standing on the wing of the fence and just took his eye off it. Whatever the cause he never took off, went straight through the bottom and really buried me. Fortina went on to win easily by ten lengths in record time. He was to become one of the great National Hunt stallions of our time. Me, I was removed straight away to hospital with a broken neck and I decided immediately that I had ridden my last race.

Once again Mercy ran the stable while I was laid up. She had always done the bookwork as she does now and we invariably buy horses together. Before we go to inspect the horse Mercy has made all the enquiries about its background and checked up all the form book details. It is the most satisfactory combination possible.

I never even rode work again after my fall on Coloured Schoolboy. At first I tried to ride a little cantering but then I used to get dizzy spells and so I decided to pack up riding all together. It was really the doctors who made my mind up for me and told me to call it a day. It was a blessing in disguise probably because I was able to stop that constant struggle against increasing weight before it had time to affect either my riding or my system.

My most difficult problem when I had given up riding was to decide which jockeys were going to ride for us. Mercy tells me that I was very tiresome. I used to get into terrible states and would jump every fence on the course with the jockeys. No-one could ride to suit me. It is the old story. If you have the best jockeys riding for you, they are not riding against you. I think today that a lot of the younger trainers have not ridden themselves and therefore are not as fussy or possibly it is that they do not know much about the art of riding over fences and hurdles.

Like my father before me, I have always been a professional and I have no time at all for ignorant trainers or permit holders with half-trained horses ridden by hopelessly inexperienced boys who don't know where they are going and will not stay straight, thereby making race riding more difficult than ever for the good professional jockeys. This has had an effect upon the type of horse involved. Before the war you could win over hurdles with a six furlong flat horse. But now you have got to be up with the leading bunch all the way to keep out of trouble, so you need one that gets one and a quarter miles on the flat.

I am a great believer in old Atty Persse's oft-stated theory: 'A jumping trainer means a man who trains his horses to jump. If they fall, you are falling down on your job.'

In 1952 Mercy and I went to America. We had earlier visited France and in both countries we saw loose schools in constant use to teach young horses to jump. We came back fired with enthusiasm and built one at Kinnersley. All the young horses and all three-year-olds go into the loose school. We put the old horses in it only as a correction. The horses school completely loose, not on the lunge. There are four obstacles. If they go round ten times they have jumped forty. I let a three-year-old canter round first to find its bearings and get accustomed to being enclosed, then I put the poles up and gradually increase the height. They go up to about 3 feet 6 inches. They are fixed and cannot be knocked down.

The horses soon come to love it. You have to stop them jumping round and round. The great benefit of the loose school is that the horse makes its own mistakes and discovers how to put itself right. It discovers the most natural way to jump properly and acquires a sense of timing which it is unlikely ever to lose. When Normandy won first time out over hurdles at Kempton, he had only been in the loose school. He had never been ridden over a hurdle in his life.

Incidentally I think it was a good idea when the authorities decided to colour the tops of the hurdles because it makes the horses just look at them. They have had far fewer hurdles broken since they introduced that orange top rail.

I believe that it is a good thing for the jockeys that are going to ride the horses in their races to school them at home. Then, as a trainer, I can see whether they are going to get on with the individual animals. If you have two riders, one will ride a certain horse on one day and the other another day, so that I can see which rider gets on the better with which horse.

If you have a very free horse, you want a man with excellent hands and if you have a big, bold horse, you want someone who is going to go with him too. If a man cannot get on with a horse, I would much rather that he says so and then let somebody more compatible with that animal ride him. If more jockeys and trainers were honest about that factor, it would be much better for all. If you don't suit a horse and you don't like him or get on with him, then don't ride him. In my riding days I was always honest with myself and with the trainers on this point.

I would think that a horse like Rag Trade, my most recent Grand National winner, is one of the most frightening rides you could have. When young champion John Francome rode him, he got off and said: 'I'll never ride him again!' Rag Trade is a big clumsy horse, but John Burke gets on well with him. He just sits and lets him fiddle, kicking him on when he is right.

I school separately from my galloping work. If you want to school in work, you might as well take horses to a racecourse for a school after racing. There is another theory that it helps to develop their hindquarters and muscles, but, if you are working on uphill ground, it does the job just as well, without the danger of overreaching from jumping too often. I do not school a lot. I have a school of two plain fences followed by a ditch and I have two flights of hurdles. There is no doubt that every time you school a horse you are taking a chance. If a horse does not jump well, then he goes in the loose school.

I like to school steadily. To go on quietly into the fences, let them be pulled back on their hocks, and to jump properly. There is no sense in galloping up there at a hundred miles an hour. It teaches them nothing over fences or hurdles. In the old days it was always considered to be the way to school and anybody that didn't like it was windy. Gerry was the worst schoolmaster I ever rode with. When he was riding schooling, he could not go fast enough. I refused to go with him, My father used to say: 'Why didn't you lay up?' And I would always reply that Gerry was going much too darned fast.

I am sometimes asked to compare my stable jockeys. I have usually said that Terry Biddlecombe was the best, but now it is hard to choose between Terry and Bobby Beasley. Tim Brookshaw and Tim Molony were both great horsemen. In 1959, at the end of his championship season, Tim Brookshaw rode the consistent brave Scottish hunter Wyndburgh in the Grand National.

As he landed over the big drop of Becher's second time round, a stirrup iron snapped. Tim recovered quickly, slipped the other foot free and rode on without stirrups shouting to Michael Scudamore on Oxo: 'Look—no feet!' He rode a memorable race, keeping Wynburgh in touch until Valentine's and then driving his horse after Oxo between the last two fences. Oxo hit the last but stood up. He came from it with a long lead, but Tim, riding like a man possessed, narrowed the gap stride by stride and got to within one and a half lengths. It was a great triumph of horsemanship.

Poor Wyndburgh and poor Ken and Rhona Oliver had to finish second three times in the National. But it's an ill wind, and the winner on that occasion was Oxo, trained by my old friend Willie Stephenson, who was also a great friend of Ken's and is now his partner in the highly successful Doncaster Sales.

Tim Molony, the tough, thick-set cheerful Irishman who was champion jockey five times was known by his fellow jockeys as 'the rubber man'. In his entire career he suffered only one bad fall, when he was forced to retire with a broken thigh at Uttoxeter in 1958. 'I've never believed in getting off too soon,' he says. 'I always reckon to ride my horse right into the ground—to the point of no return—you don't have so far to fall.'

That is all very well. Tim got away with it. But in the days when I was riding, a number of jockeys who followed that theory acquired the habit of staying too long and getting stuck to the saddle with the result that they were liable to have the most appalling falls because they did not allow themselves to be thrown clear.

Tim's brother Martin, a great stylist and a fine jockey on the flat as well as over obstacles, was riding for Dorothy Paget one day. In the paddock the old girl, wearing that famous grey coat and the little blue hat, puffing away at her cigarette in its long holder asked: 'Molony, will he win?'

Martin answered: 'Ah, sure Ma'am, he'll win if he's good enough and if he isn't, then he'll get beat.'

Martin rode two nice winners for me on a decent old horse called Abbot of Knowle, which was well fancied and so earned him a really good present. I telephoned him and asked him if he was going anywhere next week and whether he would come and ride the old horse again. Martin answered: 'I can't come.' He wouldn't tell me why. I wondered if someone had upset him and so I telephoned Tim and asked him to ride the horse.

I said: 'I don't understand that brother of yours. I've asked him to ride. He's won on him twice and has had a bloody good present each time but he won't come over and ride. What's the matter with him?'

Tim said: 'He's going to see the Pope.'

I said: 'Fuck the Pope!'

Tim said: 'Don't fuck the poor old Pope. Martin would never forgive you!'

The first winner we trained from Kinnersley was a horse called Good Date. We had just moved in and a number of friends had been telephoning pulling our legs a bit. After racing one evening we were laughing and joking, drinking with a few owners and neighbours when the telephone rang. A voice said: 'This is Paul Munster.'

'Who?', I shouted.

'Paul Munster. Count Paul Munster.'

'Oh yes?' I said. 'And my name's Lord bloody Fred Rimell!'

It took some time to sort it out but I eventually discovered that he actually was an Austrian Count. A hell of a nice chap and a good owner, he sent us Good Date and we won a race with him before he sold him on. Sadly, Paul is dead now.

Two horses must vie with Coloured Schoolboy as the best we trained in the early days. At Newmarket Sales we paid only 410 guineas on behalf of our first owner Frank Jordison for a gelding by Flag of Truce out of Scotch Widow, which he very neatly named Unconditional Surrender. He was a grand sort of horse with the soundest of limbs but as a youngster he was plagued with sore shins. Eventually we managed to get him on the course in a maiden hurdle at Windsor. I was still riding in those days. He ran so well that Ron Smyth came upsides as we pulled up and said: 'Mate, that'll do. I don't want to know when it's off. I just want a tenner on it!'

He went straight over fences and continued running and winning to a ripe old age. At the end of a long and honourable career he was retired. Frank Jordison met that popular stipendiary steward Tom Holland who said: 'I hear you've retired your old horse, Mr Jordison. What a wonderful chap he has been.'

'Yes,' said Frank. 'He has won thirty-two races and has been placed many times and he wasn't fancied on two occasions, but won them both!'

We bought Comique for only 300 guineas, also at Newmarket, out of Jimmy Rank's stable. He had been a very good two-year-old but they had raced him hard, too hard, so that he was useless as a three-year-old and they outed him. He was a windsucker and a crib biter. We did not attempt to stop him, but took everything off him and just let him do it. The secret was that we would just tie him up short for only about an hour before a race so that he would not get at the manger. He won thirty-four races for us. A super horse, he belonged to an undertaker down in Devon. I rode him one day at Newton Abbot and noticed that the tide was up. Now even in high summer when the ground is firm this has the effect of making one part of the course like a bog. There was water lying in the usual place on the home turn. So I went down in the morning and cantered Comique twice through this water. They all thought I was mad. When we came to go round in the afternoon, he went through the water like a duck, and all the other runners were floundering not knowing where on earth they were.

Coloured Schoolboy raced on happily after my retirement from riding. Ridden for us by Tim Vinall, he finished third in the Cheltenham Gold Cup of 1948 and '49. There was one big stumbling block at that time. Vincent O'Brien had the brilliant Cottage Rake and those two years were the first of his Gold Cup hat-trick.

We were now building up a stable of good owners and good horses. Some of the most sporting businessmen in the world live within striking distance of Britain's second biggest city, Birmingham. They work hard and play hard. They love their hunting, shooting, fishing—and racing. When they come into racing, they like to have their horses close to home, so that they can come down, watch them work, have a drink and chat about them. It makes all the difference. For these people, who live within striking distance of Birmingham, we are, of course, ideally placed. Add the sporting farmers and landowners of Worcestershire and Warwickshire, and you can see how we were able to build up a magnificent clientele. Unfortunately one of the saddest things about training is that so often you cannot win for the best owners, but have unending success for the ones who do not come into that category. Mercy and I have often discussed this point. She thinks that perhaps one is inclined to try too hard to buy the right horse for the best owners. Whatever the cause, nine times out of ten it just doesn't work out. Yet the good owners will go on year after year despite all their bad luck, where the other type would have chucked it up a long time before if they had not had so much success.

In addition to horses and owners we were building up a staff who were to stay with us for a very long time. Ron Peachey, whose father was stud groom to Lady Wyfold for forty years and who had thus been born on that famous stud, served in the Coldstream Guards and then came to us at Kinnersley in 1949. For a short while he did his two, then he learned to drive the box and soon became head man. He married Mick, the girl who worked in the office for my old man before the war and has been our secretary ever since. It is the happiest and most efficient set-up imaginable.

One of the best and shrewdest young trainers today, Barry Hills, started his life at Kinnersley where his father, Bill, was head man for my father. One day we had an urgent summons to the Pony Club camp where our son Guy had taken Barry who was staying with us here. Mercy had to remove them both because they were considered uncontrollable and had been chasing the girls around the dormitory all night!

There was another incident one day when my head man, Ron Peachey, was driving the horsebox. Barry was travelling with the horse and Peachey told him: 'We will stop some way up the road so that you can travel in the front. As soon as we're out of view of the Guv'nor you can come and jump in the front.'

While they were going up over Defford Common, they met a big lorry carrying hay coming down the road and Ron, who knew the driver well, pulled up to have a talk with him. Barry, thinking that Ron had stopped for him to climb into the front, leapt out of the back. Just as he was running from the back to get into the front of the box, Ron waved goodbye to his friend and drove off. Ten miles down the road he stopped to let Barry jump in the front, but of course there was no Barry. He was walking about on the Common at Defford!

Kevin Bishop has been with me for twenty-five years and Jack Kidd, too, celebrates his jubilee at Kinnersley this year. The odd eyebrow is apt to be raised by people who are accustomed to smart, superior head men, when they see our Jack shambling along with his Northern Irish accent, untidy hair and ready grin. But I would back him against all the others any day. He is as shrewd as they come, a tireless worker, and always good for a laugh.

Jack is a lucky and successful punter. I know little about the flat form. So, when at a Doncaster mixed meeting I saw Jack shuffling off towards the bookmakers I shouted: 'What are you going to back?'

Jack's nose was buried in his card. He lifted his head, looked at me, and said: 'Now when did I last see Gloucester?' I said: 'I expect when you came through it on your way back from Chepstow the other day, you silly old bugger!'

Jack laughed and shuffled off towards the bookmakers. I backed something that is still running. Gloucester won comfortably at 10 to 1!

Jack came to me in a typical way. I put an advertisement in *The Sporting Life* for a travelling head man/box driver. The day that it appeared some of us had gathered in the little bar in the back room after racing and were putting back a few toddies when the telephone rang.

'This is Jack Kidd speaking.'

'Who the hell's Jack Kidd?' says I.

'Jesus, Guv'nor, if you saw me, you'd know me!'

'Well, what do you want?'

'I'm applying for the job in *The Sporting Life*.'

So, stuck for words, I asked: 'What can you do?'

'Jesus, Guv'nor, there isn't anything I can't do!'

'You're my bloody man, then. When can you start?'

'I'll be with you tomorrow.'

And sure enough he flew to Staverton from Jersey the next day and he has been here ever since.

Training horses is not, however, one long round of parties and big winners. It is a full-time job, seven days a week, and the 'phone never stops ringing. There are many more disappointments than there are successes, and for every big achievement that is gained, one has had to suffer innumerable heartaches, setbacks and worries. One's social life can be extremely limited as a trainer really cannot afford to leave his yard more than is absolutely necessary, no matter how competent and reliable his staff may be. The selection of races is another reason why it is so necessary to remain on the spot. One declares the same horse to run in two, or possibly three races during the week, and when you see the four day declarations you select the most suitable race.

A trainer is also obliged to travel a great deal, to and from meetings, driving many miles in a single day which becomes extremely tiring, especially as one only has three weeks' holiday per year as the jumping season lasts ten months. But it is worth every ounce of effort and time devoted to the job if one is able to bring a horse to the racecourse 100 per cent fit—especially if he then wins!

VIII A First Ace

Among our owners at this time were the Oliver brothers, whom I mentioned earlier. Rowley and Harvey had inherited a lot of money from their cattle-dealing father and lived life to the full on their land around Droitwich.

It is easy to be wise and critical about other people's troubles. Suffice it to say that they overspent in many directions and gambled unwisely. But they were good friends and good owners. We bought them some fair horses, including the good chaser Land Fort whom we found for them in Ireland.

Mercy's mother was always highly successful in the show ring. Over the years she had some exceptionally good show horses which won all over the country including the biggest shows like the International and the Royal.

In the summer of 1949 she went to see an unbroken three-year-old by the French sire Bidar out of English Summer, which was running out in a field near Lapworth in Warwickshire. Funnily enough this field adjoined the land of Mr and Mrs Leonard Carver, very keen horse people, who had thus been looking at him since he was a yearling over the hedge and had done nothing about it. He was unbroken and my mother-in-law was inspecting him with a view to buying a show horse.

After she had seen him she came over to Kinnersley and said: 'I have seen the most lovely horse. I know nothing about him but he is a really beautiful animal. For me he is just a tiny bit pin-toed on his off fore which would stop him as a show horse but I think that you two ought to go and look at him, he's got more than a touch of class about him.'

When there is a promising horse to be bought, we have never let the grass grow under our feet. We jumped in the car and went over to see him. As soon as we set eyes on him, a lovely dark bay, we fell in love with him. He had been bred in Ireland and bought as a youngster by his present owner Mr Blackstead from whom we now bought him for £1,750 on behalf of Rowley Oliver. He was named ESB.

Back at Kinnersley we were delighted with our new purchase. As we started to break him and he was pulled together by the tack, he improved even more. Not only was he that wonderful rich genuine colour, but he had a lovely quality head with good big ears and a bold eye. He had great depth through the heart, a fine spring of rib, powerful quarters and a good straight hind leg with a strong second thigh. He gave the impression of power, quality and balance.

As soon as we had broken him, we taught him to gallop and he took naturally to jumping.

The first time that ESB won at Wincanton on Boxing Day, ridden by our apprentice, he was very well backed by his owner Rowley Oliver and started at 8 to 1. Unfortunately Rowley had neglected to tell his brother Harvey, for whom we trained those good horses Land Fort and Abbot of Knowle, that he thought ESB would win. When I got home that evening after Wincanton, I discovered that both Land Fort and Abbot of Knowle had disappeared. Rowley telephoned in a terrible state. He said: 'Harvey has taken the horses and turned them out in a field somewhere. I expect that they are somewhere around here at Hartlebury. Don't worry. I'll find them and call you back so that you can come over and collect them with the box.'

It was a freezing cold December night. Hardly the time to turn out high mettled racehorses in full training.

At one o'clock in the morning Rowley telephoned again and said: 'I've found the horses. If you come over in the box with a couple of lads, we'll be able to catch them.'

So over we went and there were Land Fort and Abbot of Knowle standing shivering under a hedge. We loaded them up and brought them back here to Kinnersley where their warm boxes were waiting for them. Five days later Land Fort won a decent race at Cheltenham.

Then we decided to go for Cheltenham's four-year-old Juvenile Chase which is now defunct. Martin Molony came over from Ireland to ride ESB in his preliminary outing over fences at Birmingham. I told him: 'Give him a nice quiet race, but I don't want a penalty for Cheltenham.'

When he came in after finishing fifth or sixth, Martin said: 'I couldn't have been much nearer, Guv'nor.'

This was disappointing, but he was still a sloppy big baby of a horse. So, when we went to Cheltenham, I put a pair of half blinkers on him and said to Martin: 'Get hold of this chap. He went to sleep with you at Birmingham.'

They jumped to the front after the water and won eight lengths. As he walked in. I went up to Martin and before I could say a word, he said: 'Ah, Jesus, Guv'nor, you were right. You were right. You were right!'

When the Olivers' financial troubles came to a head, Rowley telephoned and told me that they would have to sell ESB.

As locals, Mercy and I had, of course, sadly seen the trouble coming and had made plans. I immediately telephoned Leonard Carver at Lapworth and offered him the horse. He was very friendly at the time with Geoffrey Kohn, rang him up and asked him: 'What do you know about this horse? Would he be a good buy?'

Geoffrey said: 'Yes, I think he would be.'

The next thing I knew was that Geoffrey Kohn called me himself and bought the horse.

There was a hell of a row between Kohn and the Carvers and they started out with a partnership which was never a very happy one. He ran for one season for them, but in those days both owners' names were not printed on the race card and so we used to make alternate entries. First Mrs Leonard Carver's ESB and then Mr Geoffrey Kohn's ESB. The idea was in theory that he should run for each of his two owners on alternate occasions. But, as everybody connected with racing knows, you do not always run a horse in every entry you make for him. If he ran in two consecutive races in the same name, there was always a dust-up about it. Both owners wanted the horse to run in their name. It was almost an impossibility. So finally they decided that the horse should be put up for public auction to dissolve the partnership.

He was sold at Newmarket. By a coincidence Geoffrey Kohn owned a very good horse on the flat, a son of Royal Charger trained by Sam Armstrong called Royal Serenade, a classic type of horse of the Nearco line, who was to prove an outstanding stallion in the United States.

How blind people were. Perspicacious Clive Graham, 'The Scout' of the *Daily Express*, whose recent death was such a tragedy for British racing, paid only 8,000 guineas for Royal Serenade to send to the States. The next horse in the ring was the gelding ESB whom Leonard Carver bought for 8,100 guineas!

Now the Carvers decided to train him themselves. They did so for a year during which he won only one race and performed well below the very high standard of which he was capable. As things turned out, of course, it was the best thing that ever happened, because they got him handicapped for me. When the horse was eventually brought back here, he was on the 10 st 7 lb mark. And ESB was as delighted to be back at Kinnersley as we were to have him. From the moment he came home he thrived. He went on to win four races on the trot when the Carvers went to Switzerland.

While they were away a number of meetings were abandoned owing to frost and snow. But at Haydock on 14th January an attractive National trial was able to be run over a distance of three and a half miles. This popular racecourse, situated exactly midway (eighteen miles) between Liverpool and Manchester, has the added advantage of two drop fences, nothing like as big as the drops at Liverpool, but nevertheless they help a horse to understand that the landing may be lower than the take-off. ESB won the Haydock race.

A later race attracted the previous year's National winner Quare Times who had been sent over by Vincent O'Brien to compete and, giving 11 lb to his rival, almost succeeded. But in a tough finish he was beaten by half a length by the big clumsy Sundew, trained by Frank Hudson for ESB's former part-owner Geoffrey Kohn.

We decided to take on Sundew in the Oak Handicap Chase at Manchester on 3rd March. ESB was due to receive 6 lb from his rival on that occasion. Tim Molony, our jockey, who had ridden on the previous day telephoned to say that it was pointless sending ESB because the ground was too heavy. I told him: 'You're too late. The horse has left.' I knew perfectly well that on that good course which like Birmingham has so sadly disappeared, the hurdle course could be heavy but the chase course still good. And so, when I arrived at the meeting and walked the course, I found it was.

Sundew led to the last fence where ESB took it up and won by one and a half lengths. This was good form and we went to Liverpool with quiet confidence.

So we came to the Grand National of 1956, which was to become the most sensational of all the sensational races in the one hundred and twenty years since the inauguration of the world's greatest steeplechase. Over the years I had learned to regard the National as just another race. An important one, of course, but just another race. After all I had had so many disappointments at Aintree and I had learned that all the nervous tension which builds up in the minds of owners, trainers and particularly jockeys before the National is communicated to the horses with which they are associated. In ESB, a superbly fit high-class jumper, already the winner of eighteen races at ten years old, I had the ideal tool for the job in hand. He had learned all about those fences which were far more formidable than they are today, in a quiet run the previous year. Now, because my stable jockey Tim Molony was committed to my old friend Willie Stephenson, I engaged Dave Dick, a fine brave long-legged Liverpool rider who had already been third on Wot No Sun and second on Mont Tremblant; although he did not normally ride for us, we believed that Dave's experience and strength were necessary ingredients and that he was the best jockey available.

But we were clearly not going to have things our own way. King George VI had died in 1952 and while his daughter the Queen had concentrated her considerable knowledge of racing and breeding on the flat after she inherited the Royal stable, his widow the Queen Mother had embraced National Hunt racing with equal enthusiasm. Her knowledge and charm had earned her the love and respect of all in the sport. In fact twenty-five years later it is safe to say that the Queen Mother has done more for National Hunt racing than anyone in the whole of its history.

She had already won races with Manicou, whom she inherited from Lord Mildmay and who was to become a successful stallion; Monaveen, who broke a leg at Hurst Park; and the French-bred

M'as-tu vu, who had run at Aintree the previous year and was in the field again. But this year she had a really serious contender in Devon Loch, a son of Devonian out of a mare by Loch Lomond, who had been bought in Ireland from Colonel Stephen Hill-Dillon and first time over fences had troubled the great Mont Tremblant at Hurst Park. He had broken down and been fired. He had obviously benefited from his rest and Peter Cazalet, the Royal trainer at the time, who had already lost Grand Nationals with Davy Jones and Cromwell, was hoping that it would be third time lucky.

Clever, powerful and blessed with a tremendous turn of speed, inherited doubtless from his grandsire Hyperion, Devon Loch was a big, quality bay chaser who came to Aintree with the right credentials. Before Christmas he had won two chases at Lingfield and Sandown and hindered by snow had finished third to Kerstin at Cheltenham's National Hunt Festival. This race undoubtedly brought him back to his peak at Liverpool where he was favourably handicapped for the National which was watched not only by his owner but also by her two daughters, the Queen and Princess Margaret as well as a group of Russian statesmen, including Mr Malenkov. On a glorious spring day the majority of people obviously hoped that they would see the first Royal victory in the National since Ambush II in 1900.

Vincent O'Brien was like a test batsman with a treble century already under his belt, poised for a record four hundred. The Tipperary trainer had already achieved a unique feat with a hat-trick of Grand National victories from Early Mist in 1953, Royal Tan in 1954 and Quare Times in 1955. He was represented now by the first two of that illustrious trio. The Irish horse Must had been backed from 100 to 9 to 7 to 1 favourite for some obscure reason—I often wonder how genuine these strange big race favourites are—and Sundew, ridden by Fred Winter was second favourite at 8 to 1. We were meeting him now on 5 lb worse terms than at Manchester.

So much emotional copy has been written about this National, that, before commenting, I will quote from the report, published in the cold light of retrospect some months later by *The Irish Horse*, the then organ of the bloodstock breeders' and racehorse owners' association of Dublin.

On the final day the Grand National—for the most coveted prize in chasing—will long be remembered for the inexplicable happening to Devon Loch. This Irish-bred chaser gave a magnificent display of jumping over the thirty formidable fences on the 4 miles 856 yards course. With a six-lengths lead in the run-in he slipped up about fifty yards from the post and was passed by the other eight runners still standing at the time. A film of the race gave the impression that he rose as if to jump an imagined obstacle, became unbalanced and sprawled.

Must, who wound up favourite, fell at the first fence as did Early Mist, High Guard and Reverend Prince. As the field settled down Armorial III made the running for the first two-mile circuit of the course, with Sundew, Eagle Lodge, Gentle Moya, Ontray, Witty, M'as-tu vu, Key Royal, Devon Loch and ESB prominent. At Becher's Brook, Sundew fell and Armorial III retained a clear lead from Eagle Lodge, Gentle Moya, Devon Loch and Ontray with Royal Tan improving from the back division. Rounding the Canal Turn, Eagle Lodge moved up to Armorial III followed by Ontray who took the lead at the third last fence where Armorial III fell. Approaching the penultimate fence Devon Loch headed Ontray with Eagle Lodge, ESB and Royal Tan close behind. Ontray failed to negotiate the obstacle and Devon Loch and ESB jumped the final fence together. Devon Loch ran on strongly into a clear lead and when he sprawled on the flat ESB assumed command for a ten-lengths win from Gentle Moya, with Royal Tan, the 1954 winner, a further ten lengths away third. Eagle Lodge was fourth and Key Royal fifth. All five were bred in Ireland.

ESB's time for the race was 9 mins $21\frac{2}{5}$ secs—only $1\frac{1}{5}$ of a second outside the record which Devon Loch might have beaten but for his unfortunate lapse. Carrying a burden of 157 lbs over the thirty formidable jumps, ESB averaged almost 29 miles per hour. In the $1\frac{1}{2}$ mile English Derby the average speed of the winner weighted at 126 lbs is about $34\frac{1}{2}$ miles per hour.

Bred in County Kildare, ESB is a ten-year-old gelding by Bidar out of English Summer, by Blue Ensign out of Parapluie. Bidar, by the English Derby winner Blenheim, is half-brother to Firoze Din, third in the 1941 Derby. All the produce of English Summer to race were winners. ESB, winner of his first chase in 1950, has since won one hurdle race and eighteen chases. Subsequent to the National he failed by only three parts of a length to beat another Irish horse, State Secret, in the three-mile Queen Elizabeth Chase at Hurst Park on 21st May.

Official details of the race taken from the Racing Calendar follow:—Grand National Steeple Chase (handicap) of £100 each, £60 if declared by 6th March, or £10 if declared by 31st January, with £6000 added (including a trophy value £500) for six-year-olds and upwards; winner received £8,695 5s.; second, 10% (£1057); third, 5% (£528 10s); and fourth, 2½% (£264 5s) of the whole stakes; Grand National Course, 4 miles and about 856 yards (61 entries, viz. 39 at £100, 9 at £60, and 13 at £10).

The trainer of the winner received a cup, value £50, and the rider of the winner a cup value £25.

Mrs L. Carver's b. or br. g. ESB, by Bidar—English Summer, a, 11 st 3 lb, D. V. Dick 1

Mr J. J. Straker's Gentle Moya by Steel-point—Laura Gay, a, 10 st 21 lb, G. Milburn 2

Prince Aly Khan's Royal Tan by Tartan—Princess of Birds, a, 12 st 11 lb, P. Taaffe 3

Mr N. A. Mardon's Eagle Lodge by Jamaica Inn—Mountain Side, a, 10 st (car. 10 st 1 lb) A. Oughton 4

ALSO:—Carey's Cottage, a, 10 st 13 lb, R. Turnell; Key Royal, a, 10 st 8 lb, T. Molony; Clearing, a, 10 st 1 lb, J. A. Bullock; Wild Wisdom, a, 10 st (car. 10 st 1 lb), Mr L. Bridge; Early Mist, a, 12 st 2lb, B. Marshall (fell); Mariner's log, a, 11 st 11 lb, R. Emery (fell); Sundew, a, 11 st 4 lb, F. T. Winter (fell); High Guard, a, 11 st 1 lb, A. P. Thompson (fell); Dunboy II, a, 11 st, Mr R. Brewis (fell); Much Obliged, a, 11 st, M. Scudamore (fell); Armorial III, a, 10 st 10 lb, J. Dowdeswell (fell); Must, a, 10 st 10 lb, R. Morrow (fell); M'as-tu vu, a, 10 st 6 lb, A. Freeman (fell); Reverend Prince, a, 10 st 5 lb, Mr C. Pocock (fell); Witty, a, 10 st 4 lb, P. Farrell (fell); Domata, a, 10 st 4 lb, D. Ancil (fell); Athenian, a, 10 st 3 lb, R. Hamey (fell); No Response, a, 10 st 1 lb, C. Finnegan (fell); Ontray, a, 10 st, R. Curran (fell); Devon Loch, a, 11 st 3 lb, R. Francis (fell on the flat); Pippykin, a, 10 st, J. Power (refused); Martinique, a, 10 st, S. Mellor (refused); Border Luck, a, 10 st, M. O'Dwyer refused); Polonius a, 10 st 3 lb, E. F. Kelly (refused); Merry Windsor, a, 10 st 10 lb, L. McMorrow (baulked).

Won by 10 lengths, same second and third.

Winner trained by T. F. Rimell

7/1 Must; 8/1 Sundew; 10/1 Carey's Cottage; 100/7 ESB, Devon Loch and Pippykin; 100/6 Ontray; 20/1 Armorial III; 22/1 Gentle Moya, High Guard and Mariner's Log; 25/1 Early Mist; 28/1 Merry Windsor, Key Royal and Royal Tan; 40/1 M'as-tu vu, Reverend Prince and Martinique; 50/1 No Response and Much Obliged; 66/1 others.

Tote (2s unit): 25s. Places: 9s 7d, 13s 11d, 21s 10d.

It is estimated that a quarter of a million people visited Aintree that famous afternoon. Most of them, full of patriotism, had seen their greatest wish denied just when they thought that it had been realised. All afternoon they had been thrilling to the prospect of a Royal victory for the most popular person in the land. They had seen Devon Loch in the Queen Mother's colours racing with ESB in the Carver green and white always up with the leaders. They had seen ESB fall back at the third last fence and Devon Loch come on in the lead. They had watched the green and white colours narrow the gap between the pale blue and beige so that the two figures took the last fence together, but then they had seen Devon Loch forge his way to the front again. I too had reluctantly accepted defeat with the resignation of every professional racing man and had conceded victory to the Royal horse. Third time lucky for Cazalet. The bad luck bogey of Fairlawne and the National had been broken at last. I turned to go down to meet my horse coming in when it happened.

Devon Loch seemed to go to jump. In other words to jump at something that was not there. He then slithered along the ground and the marks of his slide remained grooved in the turf. He came to a complete stop with his forefeet stretched in front of him, and his hind legs lagging in the rear. Mercy and I screamed with delight. We could not have been beaten by a nicer person if we had to be beaten, but now we were going to win our first Grand National. Dave Dick, who had only just dropped his hands accepting inevitable defeat, quickly realised the situation, picked ESB up and drove him past the post ten lengths clear from Gentle Moya and Royal Tan.

We must have been the most neglected National winners of all time. The press went mad about Devon Loch and completely ignored us. Typical was the comment of dear old Norman Pegg, 'Gimcrack' of the *Daily Sketch*, a splendid tough old journalist. 'I've never seen bad luck like that which robbed the Queen Mother's grand chaser Devon Loch of the 1956 Grand National when he was thirty yards ahead of his nearest challenger ESB and had only twenty yards more to travel to reach the winning post.' A splendid journalist, but a little unkind to use exaggeration for the sake of effect!

All sorts of fantastic explanations have been offered for Devon Loch's collapse. Newspapers and newsreels almost all favoured the theory of a 'ghost jump'. They said: 'He tried to jump the water jump which he saw out of the corner of his eye.' They printed strips of pictures and slow motion bits of film to prove their theory. Dick Francis himself favoured the idea of a sudden rare attack of cramp—after all Devon Loch was shattering the all-time course record for that stiff four and a half mile marathon—but then decided that the collapse was more likely due to the fantastic roar of that huge crowd greeting the Royal victory. The shock wave of sound could have affected the horse dramatically.

Me, I am a realist, an experienced horseman and horsemaster. I believe that Devon Loch suffered a spasm or heart attack. I think he was like long-distance runners who suddenly do not know where they are. He was affected by lack of oxygen. And, although he was to win more races. I was more firmly convinced than ever that he had a heart condition when I saw him swerve right across the course under pressure at the finish of a race at Sandown the following season.

Anyway ESB, and not Devon Loch, had won the Grand National. I may be a bit of a rebel on this subject, and I fear that few will agree with my conviction that I ought to have won the race in any case. I was summoned to the Royal box to be congratulated by the Queen and her mother, who showed no signs of the bitter disappointment that she must have felt. But, after commiserating with her, I said: 'You know Ma'am I would have been terribly unlucky if I hadn't won because I made a terrible mistake at the third last fence. When Jack Dowdeswell and Armorial fell, I walked all over him and the horse. I was reduced to a trot. I got upsides again at the last but I had finished up my reserves in getting there. If ESB hadn't been so badly interfered with, I am not saying that he would have definitely won, but I tell you what Ma'am, he'd have been very close. It must have cost him at least fifteen lengths.'

The saddest character in the whole affair was deemed to be Dick Francis, who had had his life's ambition snatched away when it was seemingly in his grasp. He ends his autobiography—'And my fate? I know it already. I heard one man say to another a little while ago: 'Who did you say that was? Dick Francis? Oh yes, he's the man who didn't win the National!'

What an epitaph!

So be it. But it's an ill wind . . . Despite his jockeys' championship, Silver Fame, Crudwell, Roimond, Finnure, Loch Roe, Mont Tremblant and all the other splendid chasers with whom he was associated during ten years at the top, Dick's place among the immortal great ones of the sport would never have been recognised if Devon Loch had not collapsed in that 1956 Grand National. Even the talent of the jockey who wrote unpublished whodunnits in his spare time would never have blossomed into a lengthening string of world smash-hit novels (earning him the title of American Crime Writer of the Year), if that Aintree tragedy which left him in tears had not ensured bestseller status in his first major book *The Sport of Queens*, which was recently reprinted in England and the United States.

If tears were shed in the Rimell camp, they were tears of joy and jubilation. We went back to The Adelphi Hotel in Liverpool to celebrate right well. And the Carvers did us proud. They put on a proper Grand National victory dinner.

I fear that parties in general are becoming fewer. Certainly those tremendous parties at the Adelphi during Grand National week are becoming things of the past. This is probably due to the ever-increasing cost of food and drink and to the growing shortage of real characters in the sport. The parties were at their wildest and best in the days when the National was held on a Friday. Then trainers and jockeys who had been tensed up for the big race were able to let their hair down and relax for once. We were tough, healthy and fit for anything. Chief sufferers during those evenings of glorious wild excess were apt to be the huge chandeliers, so beloved by the hotels which were constructed regardless of cost in Victorian times by the great private railway companies, the famous glass fountain and assorted items of furniture, so that some of the bills presented and paid on Saturday's hangover morning were astronomical.

The knowing ones remembered not to put their shoes outside the bedroom door for cleaning. The Adelphi has two hundred and eighty-four rooms, many of them doubles. One year in the early hours of Saturday morning, about four hundred pairs of shoes were collected and thrown out of the window higgledy piggledy on to the pavement of one of Liverpool's busiest streets. A great many people were very late getting to the races!

So many memories. There was the night when the party was really swinging and the winning jockey, a large plump Irishman, approached the little Jewish bandleader who was dancing up and down in front of his orchestra.

'Would you please play "A Long Way From Tipperary"?' asked the jockey.

The famous bandleader replied superciliously: 'We don't play music like that.'

'What did you say?'

Somewhat unwisely the bandleader lisped scornfully again: 'I said we don't play that sort of music.'

'You don't, don't you? You bloody well do, you know!'

With that the jockey unleashed a hefty right hook and the bandleader sprawled on his back in the shattered chaos of his own drum kit. After repairs had been effected the orchestra played 'A Long Way From Tipperary', 'Galway Bay' and 'When Irish Eyes Are Smiling' a number of times!

Anyway we had a grand celebration after our first National and we took ESB home the next day to a hero's reception at Kinnersley. It is usually considered difficult to bring a horse back to jumping park fences in the same season as his Grand National. This was particularly so in those days when the fences were that much bigger, straighter and tougher than anything they were likely to meet on any other course in the world. I was determined to prove this wrong and took ESB to Hurst Park on 21st May for the last important event before the June/July break, the three-mile Queen Elizabeth Chase, which was the forerunner of the Whitbread Gold Cup. This had attracted seven top-class chasers including Galloway Braes, a Gold Cup winner, and State Secret. Amber Wave and Galloway Braes disputed the lead until five fences from home where State Secret went to the front. Despite his recent run at Aintree, ESB was upsides with State Secret, to whom he was giving 11 lb, as they jumped the last fence and actually took a slight lead on the run-in. However State Secret fought back, regained the lead in the last five hundred yards and was three parts of a length to the good at the post. I was very proud of this achievement.

We had only five years to wait before our next Grand National triumph. The nicest horse that we have ever won the National with is Nicolaus Silver. He was certainly the best jumper, a real precision performer who never touched a fence. He would have won any lightweight show class. A perfect mover who never would have been beaten in the show ring, if you rode him down the road he would spook at everything in the hedge, giving the lie to the theory that horses that shy are not good Aintree performers.

It is sad how many perfectly decent young men—and women too—seem to have to go through a bad period these days. Jeremy Vaughan's lasted longer than most. We had known him for many years because his father, Major Douglas Vaughan, had horses with Gerry. In the Grand National of 1948 their First of the Dandies, ridden by Jimmy Brogan, father of Barry, was narrowly beaten by Sheila's Cottage. Jeremy, a tall, sympathetic young man, who at this stage of his life like so many of his contempories was great fun until he drank more than was good for him, had always wanted to have a horse in training. He desperately wanted to go one better than his father and win the National. To this end he never stopped nagging us to find the right animal.

One day we looked in the Goff's sale catalogue for Ballsbridge in Dublin. There were only two horses in it which Mercy thought were of any interest, Nicolaus Silver and My Flame. I was racing in the north, so we arranged that Mercy would collect Jeremy at Wolverhampton races and we would all meet up in Dublin. When Jeremy arrived at Wolverhampton, he was already much the worse for wear and continued the process in the racecourse bar. Mercy, who has always been an outstanding driver, had the most appalling journey from Wolverhampton to Liverpool. She was trying to drive through thick fog with Jeremy sitting in the car snoring beside her. Grumbling quite excusably all the way, she finally got to the airport and of course, as soon as they arrived there Jeremy ordered himself another vast quantity of alcohol. She was so thankful when they arrived at Dublin and got off the plane to find me waiting for them.

The next morning we went to the sales and made a bee-line for the two horses Mercy had chosen. My Flame was out of the question. He was far too small; a pony. But Nicolaus Silver was gorgeous. The moment we saw him we fell in love with him. It was a genuine sale, because Jimmy McClintock had died and, for the umpteenth time in my life, I was so grateful that Mercy had done her homework. If others had known, as we did, thanks to her, that this lovely quality grey horse was qualified for the Grand National, I am sure that we would not have been able to buy him.

On the other side of the ring I saw Ivor Herbert talking earnestly with one of his film executive owners and I pointed them out to Jeremy. 'That is our opposition,' I said. We talked it over and decided that we would go to 2000 guineas. That was just about all Jeremy had. When the bidding opened it rose to 2000 guineas and there was only one other bidder besides us. The Irish would not have the horse at any price. Mercy and I have long been wise to the art of getting on to exactly the right figure as you get near the end of an auction sale. I managed to get my bid to 2,500 guineas and, while Jeremy whispered desperately in my ear 'That's it. Not another penny piece!', the hammer fell and the grey horse was ours.

Jeremy was delighted. In those bars at the Dublin sales which have now been moved to a splendid new ring at Kill in County Kildare, they have always traditionally had a large supply of sausages which form the staple snack and provide blotting paper for the immense amount of alcohol that is inevitably consumed. Jeremy never stopped eating them after the sale. He must have eaten 2 lb of hot sausages. As we stood there watching him, Paddy Sleator came up and we said to our old friend, 'Well, what do you think we've done?'

Fred and Mercy with Nicolaus Silver.

Nicolaus Silver and Bobby Beasley, winners at the last fence of the 1961 Grand National. (*Sport & General*)

Terry Biddlecombe riding Woodland Venture in the 1967 Cheltenham Gold Cup which they won. (*Sport & General*)

Normandy (Terry Biddlecombe in check cap) coming to win the Irish Sweeps Hurdle in 1969. Persian War, third in the picture, finished third.

Normandy, Fred and Terry—triumphant after the Sweeps.

Gay Trip, ridden by Pat Taaffe, taking the last fence to win the Grand National at Aintree in 1970. (*Sport & General*)

Fred Rimell leading Gay Trip and Pat Taaffe into the winner's enclosure after their victory. (*Sport & General*)

Terry Biddlecombe, Fred Rimell and Sir Martin Gilliat, Private Secretary to the Queen Mother, enjoy a chat.

Bill Smith, now the Royal Jockey, who rode for the Kinnersley Stable. (*Sport & General*)

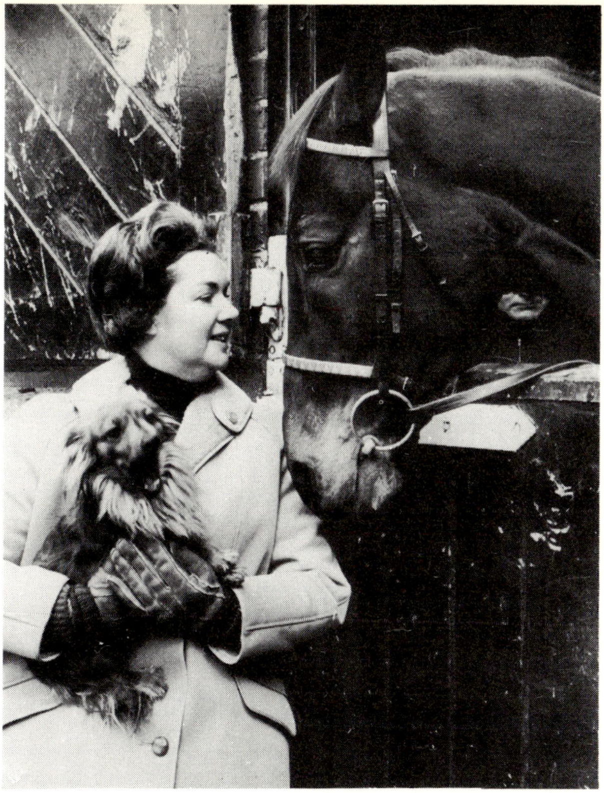

Mercy having a quick word with Pick Me Up.

Fred and Mercy attend the Queen Mother's birthday party, 1975.
(Desmond O'Neill)

Fred Rimell gives Comedy of Errors a 'well done' pat after winning the Champion Hurdle, Cheltenham 1975. (*Sport & General*)

Comedy of Errors, ridden by John Burke, takes the last hurdle to win the National Spirit Challenge Trophy, Fontwell 1976. (*Sport & General*)

Fred Rimell with Royal Frolic after the Cheltenham Gold Cup, 1976.
(*Provincial Press Agency*)

Royal Frolic, ridden by John Burke, taking the last fence to win the Cheltenham Gold Cup, 1976. (*Sport & General*)

Rag Trade, with John Burke up, gets home by two lengths from Red Rum (Tommy Stack) and Eyecatcher (Brian Fletcher) to win the 1976 Grand National. (*Sport & General*)

Rag Trade and John Burke are led into the winner's enclosure after the 1976 Grand National. (*Sport & General*)

Paddy said, 'You've given too much money for a bad horse.'

We brought Nicolaus back to England and were even more pleased with him when we got him home. He was already fit when we bought him at that November sale. The first time we ran him was at Windsor on terribly heavy ground which he hated. Tim Brookshaw rode him for us and he ran well enough to finish in the first three. As he dismounted, Tim said to Mercy: 'This horse will win a National. Put him on some good ground and he will love it.'

We ran him two or three times after that, always in atrocious going, and engaged the young champion Irish jockey Bobby Beasley to ride him in the National as soon as we heard that Bobby's chief employer Paddy Sleator had scratched his only National candidate Clipador.

Bobby rode him first on 31st January when he finished close up third after making one bad mistake. He gave him a good feel and it was obvious that he could be improved. At Leicester a fortnight later, although we finished only sixth, he was jumping those big black fences with a precision that gave us confidence for negotiating Aintree. Back at Kinnersley Nicolaus was a very happy horse and I kept him happier by putting Mercy on him. I knew he was a hard puller. Mercy has beautiful hands, but nine-year-old jumpers who have been ridden by all sorts of different lads and partnered in their races by an assortment of jockeys have been 'jobbed' in the mouth so many times that good hands are often not the answer, as they are with a light-mouthed puller on the flat. You need the sheer strength of a man. So I gave Mercy the additional aid of a double bridle. She has always fancied her chance on a handsome grey horse—with justification. They make a marvellous combination.

But every now and again, as we indeed wanted, Nicolaus, despite the double bridle, nearly got away with her. This was ideal. It made him feel a helluva chap.

Both the two jockeys that we were using at the time had committed themselves to someone else. Stan Mellor felt duty bound to ride a very much more fancied horse for George Owen, with whom he had started, and Tim Brookshaw had agreed to ride for someone else. So we decided to engage Beasley, the young star jockey with the great family tradition who had already won the Gold Cup on Roddy Owen and the Champion Hurdle on Another Flash. Even Bobby was not too keen when he was first booked for Nicolaus Silver and had been tempted to take the ride on Siracusa. And Paddy Sleator hadn't helped matters when he told his jockey: 'I thought that a very dear horse when Fred Rimell bought him at Ballsbridge!'

For the first time since Nicolaus had arrived from Ireland the going came right for the National Hunt Festival at Cheltenham. I saddled Nicolaus Silver for the Kim Muir Memorial Chase, an amateur riders' race. Ridden by Bill Tellwright, he jumped beautifully and won very easily.

We had a couple of scares before that National. A French girl came round the yard at Kinnersley pretending to be a potential owner. She obviously noted which box Nicolaus Silver was stabled in. But I spotted her at Stratford races with some characters whom I knew to be highly undesirable and reported the fact to the authorities before going home and swopping Nicolaus Silver with another grey horse. Sure enough the dopers broke in and got at the other horse but Nicolaus was safe.

Jeremy Vaughan had gone off for a holiday in Spain when I gave Nicolaus his last really serious bit of work. I sent him along with two horses, one to take him a mile and a half and the other to jump in and take him the last half mile. They were useful animals, but he scuttled the pair of them. We sent Jeremy a cable to tell him that the horse had gone wonderfully well and had put up a marvellous gallop. At that time the price was about 66 to 1 and I'm happy to say that he stood to win a lot of money over the horse.

The second scare came two days before the race. My head man Ron Peachey reported that the horse had been shod on Thursday ready for the race, but that later in the evening they had noticed that his left foreleg was swollen and inflamed. Then we discovered that a nail had gone in close to the quick. We poulticed his foot, bandaged it and nursed him throughout that night. On Friday when we sent him off to Liverpool, he was still not completely sound. It was only a matter of hours before the race that he was given the all clear.

Nicolaus Silver had only 10 st 1 lb to carry. So Bobby would do the weight easily with a nice comfortable 5 lb saddle, which makes all the difference in a race of four and a half miles over those fences.

When I saw him again on the eve of the Grand National at Liverpool, I knew that I had chosen the right jockey. He rode Fulke Walwyn's Anzio beautifully to win the Coronation Hurdle and, although that night there was a dinner and dance at the Adelphi, at which most of the jockeys in their dinner jackets were enjoying themselves, he had a quiet dinner and went to bed at nine o'clock. He was still at that time a dedicated fitness fanatic, smoking and drinking very little, walking and running a lot.

Bobby had not long been wedded to Shirley Thompson, daughter of the tough northern jump jockey Arthur Thompson, who had won the National on Sheila's Cottage in 1949 and on Teal in 1952 for his Guv'nor Neville Crump. Arthur gave his son-in-law some useful tips, advising him to keep to the inside all the way where there was no crowding. 'The drops may be bigger,' he said, 'but you should have a clear run because most jockeys will try to stay in the middle for that very reason.' He also told Bobby when to give his horse an easy time and when to ride him hard.

Arthur, who still farms in Wexford, was a hard, tough, mightily effective rider with a Yorkshireman's sense of humour. When I met Bobby recently he told me a story which has kept me chuckling ever since.

One day a little northern course with a river running beside it—Rothbury I think—was honoured by a visit from the great Royal jockey, Arthur Freeman, son of the famous huntsman Will Freeman. Now Freeman, who won the 1958 National on Mister What, was Royal jockey only because he was stable rider for Peter Cazalet and I fear that, although a confident performer, he was not as great a jockey as he thought himself to be. But no-one could ever accuse him, despite his comparative youth, of being backward in coming forward. In the changing room before racing he was laying down the law to no mean tune and there was no doubt that he considered northern jockeys to be considerably below the standard of those in the south and in fact mere tulips.

The Cock of the North, Arthur Thompson, sitting in his corner, listened and said nothing.

In the first race Arthur Thompson lay handy just behind Freeman on the favourite until they approached the sharp turn by the river. Now he drew upsides with the young paragon and, reaching out his hand as they galloped along, quietly removed the other's bridle from his horse's head. This he handed to the stupefied Freeman saying: 'Yours I think!' before turning his own horse sharply to the left and going on to win the race. Freeman, with no hope of controlling his horse, sailed merrily on into the river for an ignominious ducking. It's a pity that some people will only ever learn the hard way.

We were more than a little surprised, in view of their terrifying efficiency in other matters, to find that the same thing applied to the Russians in the world of the horse. This was the year chosen by the Russians to take on and crush the effete Western capitalists at their own sport by sending over the three best chasers behind the Iron Curtain to challenge for the Grand National. They were called Grifel, Reljef and Epigraff. What was considered by some to be a courageous sporting venture was in fact, owing to lack of any proper reconnaissance, the most stupid enterprise imaginable, doomed from the start to end in humiliation. At the end of their five days' journey across Europe, we were introduced to three horses and their riders, who, despite their successes behind the Iron Curtain, were all clearly about the standard of middling point-to-point performers. Yet they had been brought to the home of steeplechasing to compete against the best human and equine professionals in the world's greatest steeplechase. Of course it was satisfying for us, but at the same time it was pathetic and somehow vaguely annoying.

The prize money for the National had jumped from £13,134 in 1960 to £20,020—easily a record and an extraordinary sum in a sport which still had steeplechases worth less than £200 to the winner. In addition to the organisers, part of the prize was contributed by the Irish Hospitals Sweepstakes and part by the mineral firm Schweppes, who subsequently received only seventeen press mentions for their money and pains, with the result that they transferred their allegiance to their own hurdle race at Newbury—a decision that they have never regretted.

The fences had been altered, chiefly in the hope of attracting top-class chasers to Liverpool and, I suppose, partly due to criticism.

In the past many horses had fallen as a result of getting too close to the big upright obstacles. Now these were sloped on the take-off side, giving a horse another yard in which to see the fence and time his take-off. The top weight had been lowered to 12 st.

Automatically on this mark, because they had not run before in England or Ireland, were the Russian horses, of whom only two went to the post because Epigraff was lame. The runners were Reljef and Grifel, ridden by B. Ponomarenko and V. Prakhov. So these animals, who were certainly the best steeplechasers from the Iron Curtain countries, but would have been pushed to win the smallest selling chase at Wye, were compelled to give weight to three previous winners of the National—2 lbs to Neville Crump's mighty Merryman II, 5 lbs to Mister What and 6 lbs to Oxo. Grifel, a golden chesnut, stood just about 16 hands; Reljef, a medium bay, was only 15 hands 3 inches. If the previous year's winner, white-faced Merryman II, standing over 17 hands and full of power, had ever appeared in a field of horses of this type, he would have looked like Rocky Marciano at a deb dance.

The riders did not even dress like jockeys. They looked as if they were going for a hack on Hampstead Heath. Half an hour after the last race on the first day of the Liverpool meeting, Vladimir Prakhov and Boris Ponomarenko stood in the weighing room earnestly asking Laurie Morgan how to ride the National course. They had just seen the Australian Olympic champion winning the Foxhunters Chase on Colledge Master for the second time. He explained to the Russians that the Chair was in his opinion the worst obstacle on the course. But they told him through their interpreter that Becher's Brook, where they had seen three horses fall, was the fence that was giving them a headache.

They said that it was the only fence they feared, and because of their concern over it certain arrangements were made for them to have 'grandstand' seats beside it for the two big races on the first day over the National fences, The Topham Trophy and the Foxhunters.

That night back at their hostel on Haydock racecourse twenty miles from Aintree, the Russians held an 'inquest' on what had caused the three horses to fall. Prakhov, Champion of All Russia, and his colleague Ponomarenko paced their long narrow dining-room reasoning out the crashes. In typically Russian fashion nothing was being left to chance—except, of course, the fact that even they must by now have realised that both horses and riders were hopelessly outclassed and overfaced in attempting to jump the Aintree fences at racing speed. After all when ESB, who incidentally completed the course honourably on two subsequent occasions, had won his National five years earlier, he had done so at an average speed for the four and a half miles of nearly 30 miles an hour, only 5 mph slower than the average speed for the Derby.

Just to show how little reconnaissance had been done, Yuri Alexiev, deputy manager of the Moscow racecourse and leader of the party said when they arrived: 'We did not expect top weight when the trip was planned, but even with 12 st we think our horses will finish the course.' And yet the least experienced apprentice would know that horses that had never run here before automatically carried top weight in the Grand National handicap. For the great race itself the riders discarded their suburban hacking attire and adopted even more way-out costume. John Hislop wrote in *The Observer*:

> When the horses came into the paddock the centre of interest was the Russian pair Reljef and Grifel. Neither looked the part for the job, being typical flat racehorses, and Reljef, a lightly-framed little bay, looked barely big enough and strong enough to jump hurdles.
>
> Both entires, they carried a bloom on their coats which geldings do not have, but neither was well groomed or well turned out. With their manes unplaited and their tails long and untrimmed, sporting rawhide bridles and a circular steel metal disc on the headpiece just below the ears, they had an oriental air about them.
>
> Reljef, who unseated his rider after Valentine's first time round, is a neat little horse with an attractive head and slightly lop ears. His stable companion Grifel is bigger and stronger, but rather plain about the head with a wall eye, a crooked near foreleg and a slight stringhalt.
>
> The Russian riders also attracted interest and attention. More heavily built than their English counterparts, especially Prakhov, Grifel's jockey, they presented a rather strange sartorial picture,

as they did not wear the usual white neck scarf used by English riders, nor the elastic bands round the wrists to keep the sleeves of the jacket from flapping about; as a result they looked as if they were wearing pyjama jackets. Ponomarenko, Reljef's jockey, wore a stylish pair of boots, their tops being of white leather with the lower edge generously waved, giving them the appearance of being part of a circus rider's attire.

So it was obvious that we had nothing but nuisance value to fear from the Russian challenge.

Although at the last moment the Irish candidate Jonjo, the mount of Pat Taaffe, was backed down from 100 to 8 to 7 to 1 favouritism, the obvious danger was last year's winner Merryman II, despite his weight of 11 st 12 lb. People talk so glibly about weight, ignoring the fact that it is relative to the horse's size. However good a small, light horse may be, it is seldom physically strong enough to carry large burdens. Merryman was exactly the opposite. A massive, old-fashioned sort, he was up to any weight and more than capable of carrying 11–12 st. On the other hand I very much doubted whether even he, grand individual that he was, could give 25 lb to Nicolaus Silver over four and a half miles. In the enforced absence of his jockey Gerry Scott, Neville Crump had approached Ryan Price for the services of Fred Winter, but a short while before the race Ryan had bought Kilmore in Ireland and, to Fred's dismay at the time, he had to ride the little bay horse. He admitted afterwards that he was highly surprised by Kilmore's performance and said that if he had known him better and had had more confidence in his ability, he would have finished considerably closer than fifth. I am glad that he had not got to know him so well!

No grey horse had won the National for ninety years, since the gentle little 15 hands 2 inches pony The Lamb had triumphed in 1868 and 1871. The Lamb was Limerick-bred and after winning a few races on the flat in Ireland, he was sold for £25, being described by one would-be purchaser as 'too small and weak to carry a man's boots'!

It was a lovely clear day as the thirty-five runners paraded in front of the stands. Bobby Beasley, wearing Jeremy's Cambridge blue, pink hoop and armlets and quartered cap on our beautiful grey horse made a pretty picture. I think that Mercy and I remember this race so vividly because it gave us more pleasure than almost any other.

There was a sensational start. As they walked up to the tapes Merryman, ridden by Derek Ancil, was kicked by Jimuru and led out of the line. But after inspection it was decided quite rightly that all was well. Merryman was put back into the line-up and showed no ill effects. In fact he was to run a tremendous race.

The ground was right on top, very fast, and before the jockeys left the weighing room, they had been warned by Lord Sefton against a mad-dash charge of the light brigade on the long run to the first fence.

So, when the tape went up, they set off at a good but sensible gallop. Nevertheless we soon knew the fate of our other runner, Floater, ridden by Eddie Harty. He fell at the first with Tea Fiend and Clover Bud. Now we had just our lovely grey horse with his flowing white tail to concentrate on. I had not muddled Bobby with any instructions and there he was, according to his plan, going quietly and steadily round the inside. As so often happens in the National one horse, in this case Fresh Winds ridden by Roy Edwards, went into a long lead early on. Next came the French candidate Imposant ridden by the leading amateur René Couetil, then Brian Oge and Irish Coffee. The leaders were the same at Becher's where we said goodbye to Grifel and Carrasco.

Fresh Winds went on in front and went further ahead of Imposant. After the Canal Turn he was a good 20 lengths in the lead. Close up behind Imposant were Vivant, Merryman, Mister What, Wyndburgh, Oxo and Kilmore. Oscar Wilde fell at Valentines's where Sibaria made a bad mistake. When the field came on to the racecourse for the first time Fresh Winds was way ahead of Imposant, with Merryman now in third position and then a bunch which included Siracusa, Wyndburgh, Hunter's Breeze, O'Malley Point, Scottish Flight, Kilmore and, to our delight, Nicolaus Silver, galloping and jumping as though he was really enjoying himself.

Fresh Winds continued in the lead but was coming back to them and Scottish Flight, Merryman and Nicolaus were closing steadily. Couetil pulled Imposant up before Becher's the second time. It was here that Nicolaus made his only mistake. Bobby said afterwards: 'He was on his nose.' But like the fine horseman he is, Bobby collected him and there was no more trouble.

When the final shape of the race began to form as it nearly always does after Becher's has been jumped for the second time, Merryman's supporters had great hopes. He was going really well in the lead, jumping boldly, accurately and fast, with no sign of weakening. When Fresh Winds fell, Merryman was left in front of Nicolaus, Wyndburgh, O'Malley Point, Scottish Flight and Kilmore. This bunch were well clear of the remainder.

As they rounded the Canal Turn for the second time and headed for home, the race looked to be between Merryman, Kilmore, Nicolaus Silver and Scottish Flight who was going well for Bill Rees. But in that unusually good visibility for Aintree we could see that Bobby was sitting with a double handful on our horse, who was still going like a train, well within himself.

Three fences out Scottish Flight made a bad mistake, but he would not have won in any case. As the runners headed for the racecourse after jumping the last fence in the country, it still looked to be anybody's race. At least that's how it looked to most spectators. We, on the other hand, were now full of confidence. Although Merryman was going as strongly as ever, our horse was moving up ominously. Kilmore was still a fighting force, while O'Malley Point was creeping up on the heels of the leaders and Wyndburgh was plugging safely along, ready to take advantage of falls in front of him.

At the second last Merryman was still in front and on the stands his supporters were beginning to cheer the prospect of the first double victory since Reynoldstown. He landed two lengths clear of Nicolaus Silver, with Kilmore almost upsides and O'Malley Point trying to join them.

Coming to the last, Bobby brought Nicolaus up on Merryman's outside to launch his final challenge. He looked quickly over his right shoulder to see if there was any danger from that direction and then he gave his full attention to getting over this obstacle, balancing his horse nicely on landing and then making the best of his way home. Nicolaus was going so easily that he had to take that fence in front and so he did, with Merryman trying desperately to get on terms. Bobby kept our horse going so strongly and the grey was so full of running, that by now there was no doubt in our minds about the eventual winner. By some strange instinct—Bobby had ridden in only one Grand National before, when he had finished seventh on the little mare Sandy Jane—he seemed to know that the middle of the course was the better way and, leaving the rails to Derek Ancil, he rode home with all the style of that beautiful rider, his father Harry Beasley, and all the pride of his grandfather, another Harry, who had won the National in 1891 on Come Away and who, with his brother Tommy, had farmed the big Aintree chase for fourteen years. Derek Ancil and Merryman fought all the way, but they had no chance against our brilliant jockey and our super-fit grey horse, who ran home past the post with his ears pricked, a most impressive winner by five lengths. O'Malley Point just got the better of Scottish Flight by a neck for third place and brave little Kilmore, eleven years old, who was to win the following year, was the same distance away fifth.

The time of the race, 9 minutes $22\frac{3}{5}$ seconds was the fastest since the victory of ESB six years earlier and was only $2\frac{1}{5}$ seconds slower than Golden Miller's record in 1934. Fourteen finished—the largest number to do so in the last decade.

I have never known any jockey as happy as Bobby. At twenty-five years old, entirely dedicated, he had won the race that he had set his ambition on, and had achieved the great treble of the Champion Hurdle, Gold Cup and National. After his sheltered Irish upbringing, he was refreshingly enthusiastic and naïve. He confirmed that the only mistake that Nicolaus had made was at Becher's the second time and he added that when coming into the fence he had shouted to Merryman's jockey, Derek Ancil, 'If I get over this, I will win.'

The Russians? Well . . . although Vladimir Prakhov and Grifel came to grief at Becher's first time, the Russian rider was determined to have his round—perhaps he had fears of Siberian labour camps!—and Grifel was sent after the field a long way behind. The others were almost out of sight when Grifel reappeared in front of the stands, made a fair old mess of the Chair, ran out by mistake onto the Mildmay Course, was brought back by Prakhov to make a double jump at the water and was then pulled up.

His companion Reljef set off in the rear of the field and was soon tailed off. The jockey was unseated at Valentine's first time round. Ponomarenko said later that a loose horse cut across him and that that was the cause of the trouble.

Surprise, surprise! The Russians have not come back to Liverpool. And I doubt if they ever will. Thank heavens there is still one sport at which we in these islands excel and can beat the rest of the world.

Jeremy Vaughan, who was just thirty years old at the time, was beside himself. He couldn't believe that this wonderful thing had happened to him. He just gawped and told the press that he had his maximum bet on his horse at odds of 50 to 1. Mercy and I were not grumbling either. We had had a nice little each-way bet at 45 to 1.

As a tribute to professionalism, I would like to quote those two splendid commentators Clive Graham and Peter O'Sullevan of the *Daily Express*, when they summed up on Monday:

> This 1961 Grand Inter-National must surely be viewed in retrospect as one of the greatest in the series, re-establishing this Liverpool classic out on its own peak as the top sporting and spectacular event in the world-wide cross-country racing.
>
> Its links with tradition were emphasised when almost-white Nicolaus Silver beat the ninety-year-old hoodoo associated with horses of his coat colour.
>
> Ace-rider twenty-five-year-old H. ('Bobby') Beasley was restoring the family name to the winning role played by his grandfather Harry and brother Tommy when they won four between them in the years 1880–91.
>
> Grandfather Harry rode Come Away (1891) and he won the Grand Sefton five times. Father, also Harry (and formerly first jockey for many years to the late Atty Persse) handled the brilliant Golden Fleece to win the top sprint at the Curragh and the big chase at Leopardstown, all within a few weeks.
>
> Latest in the line, the youngest Beasley has also shown his skill in both spheres by heading the combined list in Ireland.
>
> It was no accident when seven horses streamed over Valentine's on the second circuit. They were partnered by—not a 'lucky seven'—but seven of the most skilled professionals in

the game—Derek Ancil, Fred Winter, Bobby Beasley, Bill Rees, Paddy Farrell, Pat Taaffe and Tim Brookshaw.

At Becher's on the second circuit the winner made his first and only blunder and was doubly fortunate to find his rider equipped with 'an old head on young shoulders'.

John Hislop said that Nicolaus Silver had that 'not easily defined but essential quality—character'. And added: 'T. F. Rimell, trainer of Nicolaus Silver, is to be complimented on the horse's appearance and having him trained to the minute.'

I will always believe that the real credit for that wonderful Grand National triumph should go to Mercy, who discovered that this unwanted horse was qualified for the race, organised everything and gave him the necessary confidence and sense of well-being by riding him out in all his work-up to the big race.

My word, we celebrated that night. It was the last really big party we had. Jeremy did us proud—while the poor Russian cavaliers made their way back to the hostel at Haydock with their tails between their legs, clearly feeling over-awed and perplexed by the whole business. Yes, we were thrilled to bits with our kind, genuine, beautiful grey horse who had jumped with such superb precision to win our second Grand National and we were equally delighted with our jockey.

Bobby, who had hitherto been so abstemious throughout his life, let his hair down and joined in the celebrations at the Adelphi with a vengeance that night. In his own words: 'I got tight for the first time', but, because he was fit at the time and had a horror of not feeling well afterwards, he stopped when he had had enough. When he is on top form Bobby is the best chap imaginable at a party and he was a real 'gas man' that night. Unlimited champagne flowed. But, for some reason, for which we are eternally grateful, Mercy and I have always been able to drink our fair share, join in all the fun and still remain sober. So I was already thinking to the future and half way through the evening I took Bobby on one side and asked him: 'How would you like to ride as first jockey for me next season? Don't try to decide now. Think it over and I'll be in touch next week.' I offered him a £1,000 retainer and a house in Worcestershire. Even today that would be a fair start for an Irish jump jockey coming over to take up his first English job. It took Bobby some time, however, to adjust to the thought of leaving the country and the life which he knew but in the end, persuaded by his young wife Shirley and by Paddy Sleator, who had already formulated plans for having horses trained in England, he decided to accept.

Then on Easter Monday I decided to jolt the purity of Bobby's little world with a joke. I telephoned a cable to the weighing-room at Fairyhouse's Irish National meeting saying: 'Can you ride Joe's Girl Woore?' and I just signed it Rimell. Apparently the other trainers and jockeys, knowing Bobby, were delighted. They never stopped pulling his leg. He said later: 'I was acutely embarrassed. It had to be explained to me that the Rimells had a mare called Joe's Girl and that there actually was an English race meeting called Woore—not Whore!'

Anyway he came over, rode her and she won. In his book *Second Start*, a frightening, moving, compelling human story of his descent into and final triumphant return from the depths of alcoholism, Bobby describes his entry into our world. I include this description here, with no apologies, because it is often beneficial to look through another's eye at what you yourself have come to take for granted.

> After jumping the Aintree fences it usually takes horses some time to re-adjust their thinking and timing to ordinary obstacles. But Fred Rimell is the exception to most rules. He put blinkers on Nicolaus Silver, wound him up and we schooled him fast over fences to such effect that only a month after his Liverpool triumph, he ran a tremendous race in the valuable Whitbread Gold Cup at Sandown and, if the going had been on top, I am sure we would have won. As it was, on dead ground, we were second, beaten only four lengths by Dave Dick on Pas Seul.
>
> Kinnersley is a few miles out of the lovely old city of Worcester. Like Paddy Sleator and Grange Con, the Rimells are the village. The house, lying just back off a by-road, is on one side of a short gravelled drive and the yard is on the other. This is not one of your glamour training establishments, but a most attractive old farm, naturally converted with numerous additions into a compact, controllable, highly efficient unit. There are

hurdles and a loose school, to which Fred owes much of his success, beside the place. The gallops and main schooling ground are across their own flyover on the other side of the busy M5 motorway. There is a modern office equipped with sumptuous easy-chairs between the house and the yard. Here, as a matter of routine, we used to meet with visiting friends and owners every Sunday morning, discussing the successes and failures of the previous week and our hopes and plans for the weeks to come. Fred is a most generous host and we always had a glass of champagne by our sides.

At first I was overawed by the whole set-up, which was so different from anything I had ever known. The green boy had arrived in a new world to an amazingly changed status as a top jockey. I found that I was treated as a friend and an equal by the top people like the Rimells. The same game, but with different trappings and trimmings. Once on a horse, I could live up to my image of a star in this big league, but although I tried to assume a sophisticated, man-of-the-world attitude, I was totally unsure of myself. I smoked more to keep my cool and drank upsides with the others to show that I was one of them.

When I turned up to ride out in the morning, I found that my horse had been made ready for me and, on my return, the lad took the animal off me as a matter of course, while I went home for breakfast, or ate with the Guv'nor and his wife. In the evenings I found we were going out to smart places that I wouldn't have dreamed of going to in Ireland.

Fred had rented us a most attractive thatched house nearby at Birlingham, a lovely old Worcestershire village.

Bobby's mention of the motorway raises an interesting point. When we were told it was coming, we were, like all country people who have been so affected, terribly worried. It was to go right through the middle of the Croome estate and divide us from our best gallops.

We were upset from the point of view of foxhunting as well. The Duke of Beaufort, 'Master' as he is known in hunting circles throughout the country, had stated his opinion that it would not be the 'antis' who would stop or restrict hunting in Britain, but the motorways. Certainly the M5 is a nuisance, although a surmountable one, from the hunting point of view. You can never risk the incredible carnage that would ensue if hounds crossed a motorway. So it has been discovered that throughout the country foxes in their cunning, just as they have taken to living in the cliffs in coastal areas, have established residence in the embankments of motorways. There they are safe. There is a theory that they find the noise and particularly the warmth of the constant traffic comforting. They can raid the dustbins in the service areas and there are very few cases recorded of foxes having crossed motorways.

From the training point of view the motorway changed our lives. Distant meetings, which formerly necessitated a day's journey across country along winding roads and in heavy traffic, giving precious horses an uncomfortable and tiring ride, and frequently meaning a night away for horses and lads, have now come to be regarded by us as local. And, from the moment that they leave Kinnersley, our horses enjoy a smooth, swift, steady ride all the way. It means too that we can return home often hours earlier from race meetings in time to satisfy ourselves that all is well with the remainder of the string, organise the work for the next day and relax in the comfort of our own house.

Jeremy Vaughan was tremendous. He was wonderfully generous not only to us but to everyone concerned. We even went on holiday together to Spain where we had a laugh a minute. Mercy and I would like to place on record what a super chap he was, and indeed is. Jeremy had his weaknesses—but then don't we all? He was too generous by half and much more sinned against than sinning. In the end happily he overcame all his problems, matrimonial, gambling and drinking which cost him a lot of money, mainly through getting into a wild set of people in London, and is now living happily at Stow on the Wold. He has no horses in training at the moment, but I sincerely hope that he will soon.

Over the years we have trained for some extremely nice people. We have been very fortunate in this, and through training for them, we have made some grand friends.

Obviously over a period of thirty years you are bound to train for a few characters that you have not liked too much and also one or two extremely difficult people. It is worth recording that, when the difficult people have moved their horses on to other trainers, they have been just as difficult in their new quarters and by and large those people have very little success in racing. The majority of our owners have been super people who left us alone and have been a pleasure to train for. For those we have been remarkably successful.

No owner should employ a professional trainer and then start telling him what to do. It is unfair and bound to end in tears. There is a lot of luck in the kind of owner that you have. I think that a young trainer starting from scratch, plagued by difficult owners, tiresome types who never leave him alone, could easily be ruined.

One of the most difficult things is to train for a businessman who is heavily involved but still wants to see his horses run. You tell him: 'I would like to run your horse on a certain day at a certain meeting. He's well handicapped, fitter than he will ever be, all the conditions are right and I reckon that he will win.'

Back comes the reply: 'Well, I'm afraid that I don't want you to run him there. I have a business appointment that day (or a board meeting or something) and I can't get away to watch him.'

He is probably a very nice person, in no way difficult, but obviously, if you have a racehorse you like to see it run and at the same time, if you have a lot of business commitments life can become a trifle difficult.

One of the questions that we ask owners when they first come to us is whether they have any preference for race meetings and whether they like travelling or dislike it. In the latter case we enter the horses nearer their homes. Others really enjoy travelling, getting away with us and making a weekend of it. They get almost as much fun out of that as watching the horse run and it is a jolly good excuse to get away for a weekend!

IX Terry

Although I was champion trainer in 1960/61 we started the following season with fairly lean prospects. This frequently happens, particularly in a jumping stable. The older horses, who had been carrying the flag so valiantly for the last few seasons and put their trainer in his lofty position, had either gone up in the handicap too much, broken down or come to the end of their racing careers. The young entries still needed time to get on their legs. You often hear trainers being praised for their patience. This is an essential quality in a trainer of jumpers which are apt to take so long to mature, and which can be ruined by being prematurely rushed. Sometimes it is not too easy to have patience because training bills are heavy and owners, who have probably laid out a fair bit of money in the first place, want to see some results. This is where real tact is sometimes needed. But the good trainer must think only of his horse and not allow any other consideration to alter his decisions.

However we still had Nicolaus Silver. After one run in the Sefton Trial at Hurst Park, we took him back to Aintree for the Grand Sefton Chase, run over nearly three miles of the Grand National course. It is a great shame that this November meeting at Liverpool has been abandoned. It gave horses a chance of running over the National fences and getting to know the course. It also provided some splendid sport and magnificent spectacles.

That year's Grand Sefton was indeed a magnificent race and spectacle in which all eleven runners completed the course. This was said to be a record. Our grey horse was always swinging along with the leaders and put in his usual stirring finish to stride home to victory by two lengths from the Irish hope Jonjo.

Bobby Beasley told me that he stood so far back at Becher's that he thought he would never be able to get over. He added:

'Although he nearly came down on his nose on landing, he was soon going all right again.'

That fine journalist, the late Geoffrey Gilbey, wrote: 'What a treat it was to see Bobby Beasley on Nicolaus Silver and Pat Taafe on Jonjo. Bobby Beasley can be ranked with such great artists as Bryan Marshall, the Molonys, Dan Moore, Harry Ussher, Jack Anthony, Fred Rees and Ernie Piggott. I write down these names as they occur to me. No one could attempt to say who was the best of these superlative jockeys.'

That victory made Nicolaus Silver the biggest prize-winner under National Hunt rules in England. It boosted his winnings to £23,377. The previous record-holder, another Grand National winner, Freebooter, won £22,498.

Nicolaus increased his winnings still further on 3rd February at Doncaster, which has always been one of my favourite racecourses. It is one of the world's finest flat and jumping tracks, a really fine, big galloping classic circuit, where all the action can be seen clearly from the stands.

I fitted blinkers to the grey horse again as I had done in the Whitbread. Although I had not considered them necessary at Aintree, they made him gallop and jump more freely over the slightly smaller obstacles. He was also lighter in condition now. It was all hard-packed muscle. He was an incredible doer and such a greedy horse that I discovered he had been eating his bedding.

Now he ran a tremendous race to win the £2,130 Great Yorkshire over 3 miles 105 yards, carrying 11 st 9 lb and jumping with speed and precision to win by three lengths in very fast time. It was a good class field of fifteen including Merryman II, Springbok and the Gold Cup hope, King's Nephew. We ran Nicolaus again in the National and we are convinced that, if the going had been on top, he would have won a second time. But heavy rain had turned the ground decidedly soft which, combined with an extra 9 lb, prevented him from finishing nearer than seventh of thirty-two behind three twelve-year-olds, Kilmore, the mount of Fred Winter, Wyndburgh and Mister What.

Although we could not know it at the time, that Great Yorkshire Chase was to be the last race that our beautiful grey Nicolaus Silver was to win. He ran for one more full season, in which he managed to finish second at Doncaster, but he had started to break blood vessels and we retired him. They say that the nearer you get to perfection, the more likely something is to go. And Nicolaus was not far short of perfection. He enjoyed a happy retirement as a hunter until his death when he broke a fetlock out with the Whaddon Chase.

Incidentally ESB was retired to the Carvers' place where he lived superbly looked after and wonderfully well in himself. We saw him not so long ago and thought he looked sensational. He had nearly reached the ripe old age of thirty when he died.

During that 1961/2 season we had one other decent horse for Bobby Beasley to ride. This was Quick Approach, a big brown horse who had come from Vincent O'Brien's Tipperary stable, where he had earned a reputation as a fantastically hard puller. One day at Ballydoyle he ran away completely out of control and ended up in a haystack from which he had to be dug out!

But Mercy, Bobby and I worked out a plan to control him. Bobby, who at the time was a very strong and fit man, would let Quick Approach take charge at the start and then pull him almost right up before the third fence. After that the horse would be perfectly all right, settling properly and allowing himself to be ridden like a good normal chaser. Bobby got a nasty shock one day when he learned the value of the Rimell partnership. He wrote some time later:

> It was riding Quick Approach that taught me the menace (or salutary effect) of TV on a jockey. I had ridden a bad race at Sandown and was deservedly beaten by half a length by Fred Winter on Some Alibi. One of the features of that glorious right-hand racecourse in its natural amphitheatre at Esher is the famous Pond fence sited on the dog-leg bend into the straight. To save ground you normally jump it at an angle on the inside corner, which was exactly what Fred intended to do as we came into it. But Quick Approach was hanging badly towards the right and I, who should have known better, tried to push my horse up on the inside of Some Alibi. Inevitably Fred jumped into the corner, cutting off my nose and I had to hook up and come on the outside. But for that, I must have won comfortably.

As I rode in, Fred Rimell, one of whose main assets is that he is always forthright and outspoken, gave me the rocket I deserved. However he is not one to harbour a grudge and, after stopping for a drink on the way home, we were good friends again by the time we arrived back at Kinnersley.

We were met at the door by Mercy. 'I had my beady eye on you,' she said sternly to me. 'What the hell do you mean by trying to come on the inside at the Pond fence? You would have won otherwise!'

Although it normally goes against the grain with a woman, you can take a rocket from Mercy. She really knows her stuff, does all the entries, book work and scheming. A remarkable woman who manages to be impeccably, stylishly turned out at all times.

Nowadays trainers can go one better. Those lucky enough to have videos fitted to their sets can show a jockey exactly where he went wrong and what mistakes he made with no possible argument.

Bobby said in that extract from his book that I am always forthright and outspoken and that this is one of my main assets. I have never believed in mincing matters and I call a spade a spade. I find it clears the air. If a jockey has done wrong, I tell him so, but equally when he has done well I give him all the praise he deserves.

One day I was at another meeting when Mercy took one of our horses to be ridden by a very fashionable leading jockey. After the race she went up to the stipendiary steward, the late John Christian, and told him that the horse should have won and would have done so if the jockey had ridden according to the orders he was given. She said: 'I know that Fred would like me to tell you this for the future.'

I was able to see the horse's next race, a much harder contest, which he won handsomely. I went straight up to John Christian and said: 'You saw that, didn't you? And you heard what Mercy told you about the other jockey's riding in his last race?' I looked him straight in the eye and said: 'What are you going to do about it?'

He seemed a bit embarrassed and eventually said that he was not going to take action. So I said: 'Right. In that case I shall have to do it myself.'

I went straight into the weighing-room, where our fashionable friend was changing, and went straight up to him. In a loud voice I asked: 'What happened when you rode that horse the other day? Why didn't you obey your orders? Either you had had a night out on the booze with the birds or you did me. Which was it?' and, without waiting for an answer, I left him looking more than a little foolish.

Bobby Beasley ended his first full English season second on the list behind Stan Mellor, in front of Fred Winter and Josh Gifford. He had had 339 rides which had produced 65 winners. Many of these had been for Paddy Sleator, who had made an arrangement for his horses to be trained in Warwickshire by a small trainer called Arthur Thomas. In fact this was purely nominal. The horses, all of them very useful performers, were trained from Ireland by Sleator who telephoned his instructions to Bobby and an outstanding head man called Jim Leigh. Thomas, who had only a few horses of his own, never set foot in the Irish yard. Now Paddy is an old friend of ours and one of the most brilliant trainers in the game. His idea was simple and foolproof.

In those days the prize money in Ireland was considerably lower than it is now and well below what it is in Britain. There were very few opportunities for all his top-class horses. But in England there are a number of condition races (as opposed to handicaps) either confined to horses which have not won a certain sum of money, or in which horses that have not won so much are allowed lower weights. So high-class Irish winners with small earnings could frequently get into a race many pounds below a vastly inferior English counterpart. It was like taking candy from kids. And, as Paddy had always liked a good bet, it was very remunerative. But in the long run it was bound to end in tears and you could not blame the Jockey Club. The situation was ludicrous. It was as though Fulke Walwyn or I had our best horses stationed permanently in Ireland or France, officially trained there by a nonentity but in fact controlled entirely by us through remote control. If anything went wrong, who would the authorities hold responsible? In the Sleator-Thomas set-up the only person whom the Jockey Club could hold responsible was Arthur Thomas, who, as everybody knew, had nothing to do with the case.

However, for the time being all went well and Bobby enjoyed a great season. But, while he was riding for Arthur Thomas, we took on as second jockey the former local amateur rider, Terry Biddlecombe. Terry was born to be a horseman. His grandfather was well-known in the show-jumping world and his father, Walter Biddlecombe, who farms the family home near Newent in Gloucestershire with his elder son Tony, has been a most successful point-to-point rider as well as earning nine victories under Rules and winning show-jumping contests at the White City and Wembley. Equally Terry was bound to have trouble with his weight. Once described as the 'Blond Beatle' on account of his long hair, he is very tall for a jockey and, although beautifully made with long powerful legs, he has big strong bones. Now, like me, he has put on a fair bit of weight in retirement.

I doubt whether any jockey ever achieved such a remarkable first success under Rules. The unknown amateur had just turned seventeen when he rode Burnella in a novice hurdle at Wincanton on 6th March 1958. He started his run two hurdles from home and, after a desperate finish, got up in the last stride to win by a short head from Piper, ridden by the great master, Fred Winter himself. It was a shattering beginning for a boy. And Terry kept it up.

He had ridden twenty-two winners before turning professional during the 1959/60 season and his first victory as a licensed jockey was Bonnie Warrior in a Market Rasen chase almost two years to the day after that initial triumph. We could still call on Tim Brookshaw, that most intelligent rider who could come back after a race and tell you all about four or five other horses. He was a very good judge and his information was a great help if you wanted to have a punt on other people's horses. Old Charlie Elsey always used to say the same thing about Edward Hide on the flat. Terry could never tell you anything about anyone but himself. He would not see what was going on around him in a race, but Tim wouldn't miss anything.

But now Terry began to get more and more of our riding and it was not long before we were delighted to take him on as stable jockey. We understood each other and the partnership was an outstanding success from the very start. The first season Terry finished up fourth in the jockeys' list; the second he was third and then in 1964/5, he took over the championship from Josh Gifford with 114 winners. He headed the list again in 1965/6 with 102. We had our best triumph at our local course Cheltenham in March 1967, when we won the Gold Cup which Arkle had made his own for the previous three years.

It had been a disastrous National Hunt Festival for the Irish and on the eve of St Patrick's Day, sun and wind had firmed up the going at Prestbury. I had never won the Gold Cup either as a jockey or trainer. This time our Kinnersley runner was Woodland Venture, a seven-year-old bay bred by popular Crewkerne farmer Harry Collins, who had run the horse in two point-to-points with no luck at all before sending him to me. He had no other horses in training.

When he arrived Woodland Venture was impossible. He refused to leave the yard and generally gave trouble until we decided to hand him over to Graham Nicholls, who used to ride for Peter Cazalet and took a pub close at hand to Kinnersley. A beautiful horseman, he rode the horse out every day, took him all around the place, opening gates and teaching him to behave like a civilised animal. Nobody else ever rode him out. But we had a number of training difficulties, a bad attack of ringworm early in the season, followed by a heavy fall in the King George VI Chase at the second last fence. At the time we were just behind tragically lame Arkle, who was making his last, most gallant, stupendous effort and, on three legs, failed by only a length to give 21 lb to Dormant.

In his next two races we found that the fall had taken so much out of Woodland Venture that we had to build him up and save him for this one great test, the Gold Cup. In addition he had to have good ground.

In Arkle's absence, his stand-in Fort Leney trained, of course, by Tom Dreaper, was made favourite at 11 to 4 with What a Myth at 3s, Mill House at 4s, Dormant at 10s, and our horse at 100 to 8.

The Dreaper cast-off, blinkered Foinavon, who, a few weeks later, was to win that ludicrous Grand National at 100 to 1 after nearly all his rivals had fallen, set off in front and led the seven-horse field for the first circuit. A cheer went up as Mill House took the lead passing the stands. I think the crowd were full of wishful thinking that the big soft bay would come back into his own now that the horse that had crushed him, Arkle was gone. But at the last open ditch up the hill, always an awkward obstacle, he uncharacteristically came to grief leaving our horse in the lead. I am quite sure he would not have won in any case. Between the last two fences Stalbridge Colonist ridden by Stan Mellor joined issue and, according to Terry, the little grey led us for a few strides. Both jumped the last perfectly, but now we saw Terry at his strongest and best. Picking the horse up, he battled up the hill with rhythm and strength, just as I remember doing myself, to win a real thriller by three parts of a length with What A Myth two lengths away third.

Terry rode for us for nine years. He has always been a generous cheerful fellow universally popular in the weighing-room. I would have preferred it if he had not ridden so short. Those long powerful legs of his deserved longer stirrup leathers. Just the same, he sat so lightly on a horse and was able to use his great strength so effectively, that it is hard to criticise. Just as they suit Lester Piggott, so the short leathers suited Terry and the idiosyncrasy was obviously no handicap to him. His judgement and timing were outstanding. He gained lengths in a race by going the shortest way. He went with his horses over their obstacles, jumping them with tremendous confidence, which is always imparted to the animal. He could pick a horse up and get it balanced again quicker than any other jockey riding when he was in his prime. He was a sensational opportunist with lightning reactions as we saw at Fairyhouse in December 1969 when he virtually stole the first Irish Sweeps Hurdle for us on Bryan Jenks' Normandy.

This was one of the four best races that Terry ever rode for us. The others were Inishmaan in the first running of the Fighting Fifth Hurdle at Newcastle, French Excuse in the Welsh National and Coral Diver in the *Daily Express* Triumph Hurdle.

When we bought Normandy, we really went over to Ireland because Robert Sangster, the boss of Vernons' pools, who has now established a turf empire all over the world, wanted to buy a jumper. He wanted a five- or six-year-old to jump fences. He did not want a three or four-year-old to jump hurdles. We went over with him in his private aircraft and Bryan Jenks said that he and his wife Rosemary would like to buy another jumper too.

So Robert picked us up at Staverton and then we went to Wolverhampton for the Jenks before taking off over the Irish Channel. Jack Doyle, the former Irish international rugger player turned bloodstock agent, who has brought off so many highly successful deals over the years, met us. There were obviously too many of us to go in one car and so we divided up into two.

We left Dublin and were soon driving across the Curragh when Mercy said to Doyle: 'Stop. I want to go and have a look at Normandy.' Jack said: 'He's too small and you won't like him.'

Mercy insisted. 'I want to see him.'

So we went to look at Normandy and, as soon as Mercy and I saw him we fell in love with him. Robert Sangster said: 'He's not quite my sort of horse and, in any case, I don't want to buy a colt.'

Bryan Jenks said: 'I don't really want him, as I have already got two of that age, Coral Diver and another decent horse.' But when I want to, I can be very persuasive, and I said to Bryan: 'Look, I love the horse. He's got good form. Bryan, you must have him.' So Bryan weakened immediately and agreed. He was ours.

Now we had arranged to go on down to what we call 'Indian country' in Ireland at the top end of Tipperary. Jack Doyle was having one of his turns, looked like death and kept wanting to stop at every chemist to buy indigestion medicine. We had arranged to be at Toomavara by half past three. It got dark at half past four. At four o'clock we still had not got there and by this time, it was snowing really hard.

So as we went through a tiny village, Jack insisted on getting out and going into the chemist to buy another big bottle to try and reorganise himself. By this time he was a nasty shade of green. So Bryan got out of the car in front and I got out too. Jenks, who is inclined to be a bit fussy, was looking around at the falling snow and said to me: 'We'd better buy a shovel.' I said: 'If you want a shovel, you'd better buy a bloody man to go on the end, because I'm not digging and I'm sure you're not!' Anyway we pressed on and I must admit Mercy and I never thought we would get to our destination. However, after going along a tiny little road for miles, we finally arrived. By that time

Mercy was bursting to spend a penny. I think we were all in the same way but it's so much easier for a man. While the rest of us were getting out of the car, Mercy hurried to the little farm, where we had been before, knocked on the door and asked the woman who opened it: 'May I use your toilet?'

She looked at Mercy blankly and said nothing for a moment or two but then she announced calmly: 'We haven't got one.'

Mercy looked at her in equal astonishment and said: 'Well, what do you do then?'

She said: 'Oh, we have a bucket in the kitchen.'

So, clearly my wife was permitted to the bucket in the kitchen. Having surmounted that ordeal, she joined us outside where by this time we were just getting out a nice-looking grey horse called Straight Boy. We bought him and, except on the racecard and in the papers, he has always been known as Bucket!

One day when he was running at Ascot and was beaten a head in a long-distance hurdle race, that smartly turned-out 'Jockey Club Lady' Mrs Jenks could be seen leaping up and down on the stands shouting: 'Come on, Bucket!' Bryan Jenks eventually gave him to Mercy who uses him as her hack. I told you earlier how she fancied herself on an attractive grey horse. Bryan Jenks was one of the best owners we ever had.

I got to love that part of Ireland and we now go over there often because Tony Dillon has made us partners in the Longfield Stud, of which more later.

Tony Dillon was probably Britain's largest wholesale newsagent. His brother is a famous Q.C. and Tony, a top-class businessman, had always had a passion for National Hunt racing. It would be impossible to find a nicer, kinder man to train for.

In 1970 we had already won a splendid flat race, the Moët & Chandon Silver Magnum over the Derby course at Epsom, which has always been known as the amateur riders' Derby. The then leading amateur Philip Mitchell rode our horse, Inishmaan, who won by three quarters of a length from Nick Gaselee on Arctic Judge.

Newcastle, one of the best and most forward-looking courses, that year inaugurated a race named appropriately, the 'Fighting Fifth' Hurdle. In October 1970 it was worth £3,973. The field, a very hot one indeed, included the already triple champion hurdler Persian War, Even Keel, the Queen Mother's Escalus and Big Valley. All these cracks were older than Inishmaan, who was still only a four-year-old. We decided that this was our race. In only a few weeks our horse would be a five-year-old. At this moment we were able to receive 12 lb from Persian War. It looked all right, knowing how fast our horse was and what a good jumper he was too.

Mercy booked Tony Dillon, Terry and me to fly from Bristol by Dan Air. When we arrived at Bristol airport, the place was shrouded in fog all around the ground; we hung about on the airport, but so did the fog. It seemed to have no intention of moving. Eventually in that horrible impersonal way that they have at airports, they announced that they were going to send us to Cardiff on a bus. Tony and Terry seemed to accept this announcement, as so many people are apt to do nowadays. We are always accepting as gospel the voice of little men in temporary authority. I think it's high time that we started to question.

On this occasion I said: 'I'm not damn well going to Cardiff. I'll try to get a private plane.' So I went to one of those charter offices and asked: 'Have you a plane that could fly us to Newcastle?'

'Yes, but we'll have to get hold of the pilot. He's in Bath.'

I said: 'Get hold of him then. I'm afraid we haven't got a lot of time.'

So we waited until the pilot arrived and came to find us in the bar. He said: 'I've just had a bit of bad luck. They've shut the door of the aircraft with the keys inside. Now they are having to take the door off!'

It seemed that the whole expedition was doomed to failure. But at long last the pilot emerged out of the fog in this twin-engined plane and we all got in. I piled Tony and Terry in and then climbed up myself to sit beside the pilot who said: 'I don't think we'll be able to take off, you know. It's very bad. We'll taxi out and have a look.'

There I was sitting in front with him while he taxied out. When we got onto the runway and he turned straight, facing up it, we could just see one red light ahead.

He said: 'You can only see one. It's not good enough.' By this time I had had enough. I told him: 'Go on. Kick the bugger in the belly. When you get to that light you'll see the next. You'll be all right, old son. Go on, have a go!'

We took off and got away with it. We had been in the air for about half an hour and the pilot had turned the heater on. It was the end of October and perhaps the plane had not been used very much since the spring. You know how car heaters smell when they have dust on them.

'I think it's on fire!' said Tony Dillon. And Terry said: 'I'm sure it's on fire!'

The pilot turned the heater off and all was well. About a quarter of an hour out of Newcastle Terry said: 'I've a ride in the first race, the novices' chase.'

I told him: 'Well, my lad, you're going to be late.' We were not going to be late and in fact, despite all the tiresome preliminaries, we were in time. But I thought that after all this fuss and bother it would be a damned fine thing to have a ride in the novices' chase, have a fall and be prevented from riding the horse you had come all this long way to ride.

So we stopped on the airport, had a couple of large brandies and arrived at the course just as the runners were going out for the first race.

The 'Fighting Fifth' Hurdle was the third race on the card. The triple champion Persian War was favourite at 5 to 2, the Queen Mother's Escalus, ridden by Richard Dennard, was second favourite at 4 to 1 and we were 5 to 1 joint third favourite with Mugatpura trained by Fulke Walwyn. Terry rode a blinder. He was always up there and, taking on Escalus and Even Keel two furlongs from home, kept a little in hand for the run-in, knowing his horse's flat speed, and got up to beat the Royal horse by a head in a tremendous finish.

They looked after us with Newcastle's own brand of special hospitality and the first thing that I knew was when we were circling over Bristol. I asked the pilot: 'Where are we?'

He said: 'We're over Bristol.'

'I can't see it.'

'Neither can I, but I know the country very well!'

And he kept circling round and round until eventually he picked up the lights and we got in.

In the first Irish Sweeps Hurdle—we seem to make a habit

of winning the first running of famous races—worth £9,457 to the winner, we challenged the dual champion hurdler, who was then a six-year-old, with our four-year-old entire colt, Normandy. Once again, getting almost to the end of the year, as we were, we were still entitled to an allowance of 12 lb from the older horse. Four days later he would be a five-year-old.

Terry rode another of his quite sensational races. He picked Normandy up between the last two hurdles and got up all the way on the inside to beat Orient War by a neck with Persian War one and a half lengths away third. It is interesting to look at the rest of that field. Celtic Gold, Major Rose, Clever Scot, Leap Frog, Avondhu, Esban, French Tan, Boatman, Drumikill, Rabble Rouser, Grand Erg and Bonne. At that time it would be hard to find a higher class field of hurdlers.

Henry Alper, the owner of Persian War, was in such a state he was insisting that he must object. He just could not believe that anything could beat Persian War. It took his trainer Colin Davies quite an effort to persuade him that an objection would avail him nothing. He had been beaten on merit.

French Excuse was a quite nicely named bay gelding by the French horse Alibi II out of Ma Poupée. As we came up to the '69/70 season, he had won four hurdle races, but he took to steeplechasing like a duck to water, and by February he was fit to run in first the Haydock Park National Trial Chase, where, ridden by our local jockey Ken White and carrying only 10 st 1 lb he trotted up by fifteen lengths. Then came the Welsh Grand National.

In this three mile six furlong race worth that year £3,314 he had earned an 8 lb penalty from his Haydock win, and now had 10 st 9 lb to carry. This was Terry's absolute minimum. He was on the 'piss pills', the diuretics, and Mercy and I have never known how he managed to ride the race of his life. He was lying up nicely when French Excuse virtually decided to take a bath in the water jump. He stopped dead and the horse, who had started second favourite at 3 to 1, was a long way behind. But somehow Terry rallied him and, coming with a tremendous run from three fences out up that switchback course, took the lead on the flat and won all out by half a length from Astbury.

Injury coupled with constant wasting is bound to take its toll.

When he literally lifted French Excuse past the post to win that Welsh Grand National, blood was pouring from his nose and he nearly collapsed.

'I'd wasted hard down to 10 st 9 lb,' he said afterwards. 'I got a bit exhausted, I'd put a bit too much into the race and, when I came in, I had cramp, felt giddy and couldn't see. I was all right until I passed the post, but when I went to pull up, my legs went weak like rubber and I nearly fell off. It's happened two or three times in long distance races. But a couple of Guinnesses afterwards, I'm flying again, especially after a win.'

Just a week later, with everything going for him, Terry had the most horrible fall of his life. David Robinson had sent us a moderate sort of horse called King's Dream; he was running a moderate race at Kempton and had no chance on the final turn, where he stumbled, hurling Terry to the ground, knelt on his back, and then rolled over on top of him. Such a stupid stumble, but utterly devastating.

When he was carried back to the ambulance on the route followed by so many of us jumping jockeys over the years to the MI hut at the bottom of the paddock, he was obviously in great pain, but at that stage we only thought that he had broken some ribs. In hospital they discovered that his kidneys were horribly bruised and lacerated. For more than three weeks he passed blood with his urine. It was particularly sad for all of us, because he had been morally certain not only to win the championship again, but also to break that coveted record number of winners. As it was, he missed nearly all the rest of the season, including the National Hunt Festival at Cheltenham. Worst, it cost him every jumping jockey's ambition, which he so richly deserved, the Grand National on Gay Trip.

This was the little bay Vulgan horse, whom we had bought with the help of Pat Taaffe in Ireland for Tony Chambers, a very old friend of both of us who enjoyed his sport and was for a while Master of the Croome Foxhounds.

It was one of those big racing luncheons at the Dorchester. We asked Pat Taaffe whether he knew of any decent horses in Ireland because we were looking for a couple, one of which was wanted by our old hunting friend Tony Chambers, who had ridden as an amateur himself.

It is hard enough at the best of times to understand what Pat says, because he mumbles so much, and with the noise of all the luncheon guests it was practically impossible. However, we did just manage to extract that the young horse he recommended particularly was called Gay Trip. So the next day we telephoned him to clarify the situation and he told us that he would pick me up at Dublin airport. However, when we arrived at the place near Naas where his owner-breeder, an Englishman called Farmer lived, we found a nice little bay horse with four huge legs like bolsters. His owner had blistered him all round! It was obviously quite impossible to inspect Gay Trip then and so, saying that I would return when the legs were fine again, I returned home.

Then Tony and I decided that we would try to find a suitable horse in France. If we were based on Paris for three days, we would surely be able to find just the right article. However, for some reason, it did not quite work out like that and Mercy says that it would probably be better to draw a veil over the whole abortive trip! She says that she does not believe that we saw even one horse! Suffice it to say that Chambers had all his money removed from one of his pockets during a night out and within two days we were coming home. Doug Francis says that he saw two very weary, jaded, dejected looking specimens at Orly Airport and suggested that we should stay on for another day, only to receive the reply: 'We're going home!' We had no horses and no money left.

A few weeks later I took Tony over to Ireland to see Gay Trip. The legs had fined down, the price was right and we knew that this was just what we had been looking for.

We backed him the first time he ran for us at Newbury but he fell at the water. Next time out he was due to run at Doncaster and I was confident that he would win. So the night before the start of the meeting Chambers, who was in cracking form, said that he would like to have £1,000 on his horse. I went up for the first day, and when my son Guy went round to Tony's house to collect him and drive him to Doncaster, he found that the owner was in a very poor way. His wife, Rosemary, said: 'He won't move.'

So Guy, all 6 feet 4 of him went up to Tony's room, pulled him off the bed and threw him into a hot bath. Somehow he got him dressed and into the car. All the way from Worcestershire to

Doncaster it was very foggy and Tony kept saying: 'Let's go back, let's go back.'

He came into the paddock just as Andy Turnell was going out on Gay Trip and asked me: 'What do you think?'

I said: 'I've put that grand on him for you.'

Tony screamed: 'What?!'

I thought he was going to have a fit. Actually I had only invested £500 for him and had had a nice bet myself. The horse won at 8 to 1 so it was a very happy beginning.

Apart from his other successes, Gay Trip won two Mackeson Gold Cups, helping to prove my theory that a two and a half mile horse is suitable for the four and a half mile Grand National.

For generations the bar fittings in pubs throughout the country had been made by the old firm of Gaskell and Chambers. John Chambers, a Harrovian who lived with his wife Hilda at Barnt Green near Bromsgrove, was a great sportsman who loved his racing. So it was natural that his son Tony should, after leaving Harrow, concentrate on trying to make himself a decent amateur. In this he succeeded, but he always wanted a really good horse.

So we persevered with Gay Trip and even ran him in the King George VI Chase at Kempton over that sharp three miles. He performed adequately, finishing fourth behind Titus Oates, Flyingbolt and The Laird. After two more outings we tried him again in the same company over three and a quarter miles in the Cheltenham Gold Cup. Once again he ran a decent race to finish fifth. This was a race that was worth remembering. L'Escargot, the chestnut, who had once been turned down by the best judges for only £600, won the jumping classic at 33 to 1.

His American owner, tall silver-haired former international polo player turned diplomat Raymond Guest, whose Larkspur won the Derby after eight horses had fallen said: 'I didn't think any horse in the world could beat Kinloch Brae and I'm sorry he fell.'

He was referring to the Duchess of Westminster's seven-year-old Kinloch Brae, trained by that little leprechaun Willie O'Grady, the life and soul of any party, who is sadly no longer with us. Their horse was favourite at 15 to 8. It was a sensational race. L'Escargot showed champion pace and was running against the advice of his trainer Dan Moore. Just as in the case of Raymond Guest's other Derby winner Sir Ivor, boldness paid off. Although

Titus Oates and Larbawn disputed the lead for the first half of the trip, and The Dikler was going well until he fell at the eleventh fence, it was Ireland's race. Kinloch Brae who had been third, jumping superbly, cruised into the lead at the thirteenth fence. Over the final open ditch at the top of the hill he was followed by his countrymen French Tan and L'Escargot, while England's pride Spanish Steps was struggling to keep in touch. Still going easily, running down the hill at the third last, however, Kinloch Brae got too close to the fence, took one stride on landing and crumpled up Thereafter it was a battle between L'Escargot and French Tan. L'Escargot won by one and a half lengths. Spanish Steps was ten lengths away third in front of Freddy Boy. The Laird was fifth and we were sixth. We were highly delighted. This was a great preparation for the Grand National in sixteen days' time.

Pat Taaffe had ridden his usual wonderful race on French Tan, despite the fact that he was now forty years old. When you have ridden all your life like Pat and me, you never seem to lose your nerve. Every race is a good hunt. So, when we came to think of a jockey for Gay Trip, we agreed with Tony Chambers that Pat, who had helped us to buy the little bay Vulgan horse, should have the mount at Aintree. Pat was every bit as good as when he had won the National on Quare Times fifteen years earlier. Gay Trip and he were indeed the class combination of the race. Pat has always believed in enjoying a really good hunt in the National until you came onto the racecourse for the last time. 'Then you can decide your inner race. Then you can start to be a jockey.'

He had Gay Trip always there or thereabouts and, passing the stands for the first time was sixth. By the time that they had turned for home at the Canal Turn fence for the last time, he had moved up two places. Poised to challenge coming onto the racecourse, he took the lead before the second last and the little bay horse galloped on well with the class that we knew he had to win by twenty lengths from Vulture.

So now we had equalled Vincent O'Brien and Neville Crump of our contemporaries. We had won the Grand National three times. Terry, who watched his substitute Pat winning the race on television said: 'It was wonderful. I couldn't have been more delighted.'

But when he came back on 29th April, still suffering acute pain from his kidneys, he disregarded all medical advice and went all out for the jockeys' championship, which had been his for the asking two months earlier, scoring his first success with Coral Diver—'the best horse I've even ridden'—at Huntingdon three days later and finally failing by only two winners to achieve his object.

When the new season started by October of that year Terry was well ahead again until he had four falls in three weeks. The last on a novice hurdler at Newbury on Guy Fawkes Day was to put him out of action with a broken back for nearly two months. But he was determined to ride Coral Diver again in his first outing of the season, the Nuneaton Hurdle at Wolverhampton four days later. Pills killed the pain, and he kept that date to win comfortably before admitting the truth of those X-ray photographs.

Mercy and I will always be grateful to Terry. After all he stands five feet ten and a half inches with a natural weight of at least twelve stone. He had to waste constantly down to ride 10 st 7 lb and collected far more than his share of injury. So much so that the *Sunday Times* published a full length picture of him in their colour supplement, annotated with his complete medical history, which, with several still to go reads:

HEAD: Concussion on over 100 occasions.

NOSE: Severe bleeding, due to high blood pressure, monthly during season.

LEFT HAND: Thumb broken 1962; finger broken 1962; thumb broken 1964; finger broken 1966; thumb broken 1969.

LEFT SHOULDER-BLADE: broken 1961; broken 1967; broken 1969.

LEFT COLLAR-BONE: broken 1964.

BACK: arthritic changes in lower back, 1966; cracked two vertebrae, 1970.

LEFT SHIN: chipped bone, 1966.

LEFT ANKLE: broken, 1966.

RIGHT SHOULDER-BLADE: broken 1961; broken 1965; broken 1965.

RIBS: one broken, one cracked 1970.

KIDNEYS: severe disorders diagnosed since 1967; two kidney stones; severe bruising and swelling.

WRISTS: both left and right wrists require extensive surgery after breaking bones on five separate occasions. Both deformed and arthritic.

RIGHT ANKLE: dislocated 1964.

All this time Ken White, a native of Worcestershire who had been born within sight of our gallops at Kinnersley, was waiting in the wings. He would never be a great jockey but he was a sound rider with good hands and an understanding of the horses that he rode. It was comforting to know that we had him in reserve for those occasions when Terry smashed himself up. Later Ken was our first jockey. Terry, like me, was fated never to win a Grand National, although, by getting Gay Trip into the frame again, he showed that as long as the horse was good enough, he was better than any of his contemporaries.

Unlike our first two National winners, Gay Trip did not meet a particularly happy end. We had him turned out to grass here and from time to time we used to take him to shows. He was a great attraction. A week after he had been shown in hand, looking magnificent, at a local hunt show, one of the boys came flying into the house and said: 'Mrs Fred, come quickly. Gay Trip's terribly bad.'

Mercy rang the vet and went straight down to the field. When I arrived, the vet had diagnosed Black's disease, which is a million to one chance and which horses apparently get from a fly. It kills them in about six hours.

By an extraordinary coincidence, the other old horse, our first Gold Cup winner Woodland Venture, was killed through exactly the same disease on his owner's farm. But this was more natural, because his owner was a sheep farmer and they say that the flies in question come from sheep, whereas there have not been any sheep on this place for umpteen years.

It was a very sad end to a great little horse.

X The Big Horse

We still have in our yard today the biggest prize-money winner in the history of National Hunt racing in the British Isles.

My first owner, Frank Jordison, telephoned me one day and said: 'I have a young fellow who lives in Birmingham, who says that he wants to buy a nice horse. In fact I think he would buy a couple of them.'

'Oh yes,' I said. 'What's his name?'

'It's a fellow called Ted Wheatley.'

'All right, Frank, bring him over on Sunday.'

Sure enough on Sunday morning a superb Rolls Corniche arrived containing Frank, his wife and this young man Wheatley. It's funny how you take to some people from the very start. Ted Wheatley knew nothing about horses, but when I got him away from the girls and into my office and asked him: 'I understand from Frank that you want to buy a horse,' he said:

'Yes, I'd like to buy a couple of them.'

'What sort of money would you be prepared to pay?'

'I will leave it to you.'

That's just about every jumping trainer's idea of heaven. But I never turned a hair—I'd always played a good game of poker—and said: 'That sounds all right. You're in business. But it's not like going out to buy something out of a shop. I will probably not find you a horse for twelve months. Don't worry. I'll be looking all the time, and if I can find any thing, I'll get in touch with you.'

Not long afterwards we were making arrangements to run a horse in Ireland in our favourite race, the Irish Sweeps Hurdle. Mercy had been in touch with a transport firm who were being rather difficult. In fact she said to me: 'They're buggering us about!'

So, fed up with them, she decided to have a word with the

Curragh Bloodstock Agency, who are also very good on insurance and shipping. She telephoned their Newmarket office and talked to a highly clued-up young man, who took the booking for the horse over to Ireland at a lower fee than the other firm, and with much more efficiency.

At the end of the conversation, Mercy said: 'You wouldn't happen to know of a nice horse for sale?'

So this young man replied that he did indeed know of a nice horse for sale, Comedy of Errors, a good horse on the flat. Mercy did not quite register immediately and said: 'Who has him? Is he in Ireland?'

This was fairly natural, because although we had won top class flat races at the great course like Ascot and Epsom with splendid old staying warriors like Trelawny and Pick Me Up, we are in the happy position of not having to keep our eye on the flat race form book. In fact, we have gone to Africa recently in the summer during our rest period, first big game shooting on safari and then shooting cameras.

So, when Mercy asked: 'Is he in Ireland?', the young CBA man replied: 'No. Corrie's got him at Shrewsbury.'

Said Mercy: 'Fred knows Tom Corrie very well. He'll have a word with him and go and see him.'

So I telephoned Tom Corrie and said: 'I hear, Tom, that you have a nice horse called Comedy of Errors for sale.'

'He is not for sale.'

'Tom, if ever he comes on the market, perhaps you will give me first refusal?'

Tom said that he would and he seemed to be messing about a bit. Anyway, I put the telephone down and was a little bit annoyed. I telephoned the Curragh Bloodstock Agency again and asked: 'Who put that horse on the market—the owner or the trainer?'

'Oh, the owner, Jarvis.'

I told them that I had had a word with Tom Corrie, who said that he did not think that the horse was for sale. And I suggested 'If you want me to see the horse, I suggest that you ring up Jarvis and make an appointment for me at eleven o'clock on Sunday morning.' I put the telephone down and set off for Cheltenham where I was lucky enough to saddle two winners myself and back three others.

But all the way through the afternoon this matter haunted me a bit. Big Tom Corrie had been a friend of mine for many years. He knows his horses and he loves a punt. He is a splendid friend. So I kept saying to myself: 'Corrie doesn't want to lose this horse. He is obviously a decent horse and he wants to train him.'

When I returned from racing there was a message on the pad in the office saying that Mr Jarvis had telephoned to say that it would be perfectly all right for me to see the horse on Sunday. I thought I had to do something about this, and so I wondered whether to ring up Tom or Jarvis first.

The form book and *Timeform* gave Comedy of Errors a fair write-up. The brown gelding sired by the sprinter Goldhill out of Comedy Actress by Kingsway had not run as a two-year-old and had been second in one of his two outings the following season.

He was described as: 'Strong gelding: has had a good season to date and been successful in maiden race in Wolverhampton and handicaps at Ripon and Chepstow: has run twice at York, finishing fourth behind Prominent in John Smith's Magnet Cup in July and occupying same position behind King Midas two months later. On both occasions finishing strongly after being well behind turning for home. Stays at least eleven furlongs, acts on any going.' That season as a four-year-old he had won over nine furlongs and twice over one and a quarter miles. On paper, at least, he was obviously a good sort of individual.

So I telephoned Jarvis and said: 'Thank you very much for your message to say that you would be prepared to sell Comedy of Errors. I spoke to Tom Corrie yesterday but he was not quite certain whether he wanted to sell him or not.'

So Mercy and I motored over to Leighton Hall near Shrewsbury, Tom Corrie's home, where he managed his stud, shot, fished and still had a few nice horses in training.

With obvious reluctance Tom brought up out of the field a big brown gelding covered in mud. When I say big, I mean very big indeed. Nowadays you don't expect a well-made thoroughbred with good performance standing over seventeen hands but this one did. He was covered in mud, where he had been rolling in his field and I suppose that many of your Newmarket or Epsom trainers might have turned him down. But Mercy and I were used to this sort of thing. We had him trotted up the road and saw him move beautifully straight. I said that we would give £10,000 for Comedy of Errors. So we went into the house and had a glass of champagne. Tom didn't have to mind: it was one of those things because the price was right for the horse and Jarvis wanted to sell.

Mind you, I had known old Tom for years as a friend and every so often I have felt a bit bad about it, particularly when going to Cheltenham with a very good chance in the Champion Hurdle.

That was not really the end of the drama because Ted Wheatley claimed that he owed most of his prosperity to his friend Harry Plotnek. So it was that I received a message from Frank Jordison saying: 'Listen. You must have a word with Wheatley. I understand that he is going to give Comedy of Errors to Harold Plotnek as a present.'

Wheatley had asked me to buy him a horse. I had done so and he was one of my owners. I owed him loyalty. So I said to Frank: 'Christ! He can't do that!'

So I telephoned Ted Wheatley and said: 'Frank has been on the phone. He says you are going to give Comedy of Errors as a present to Harry Plotnek.'

'Yes. This is a fairly involved affair and you don't understand. He has been a great friend of mine and has helped all through my difficult times and, if it was not for him, I would not be where I am today.'

I said: 'Ted, this is the nicest horse that I have ever found in a long, long time. I don't know your friend, but I'll buy the bugger another horse.'

Eventually I said: 'All right. So you want to do him a favour, well, you can't bloody well give him the whole horse. I wouldn't be doing my job for you if you did. You can give him a half share.'

'I'll do that.'

So that was how Wheatley and Plotnek came to be partners in the same horse.

He was a huge magnificent animal with great spirit, and, when we got him home to Kinnersley we schooled him first in the loose school and then over hurdles. He jumped really well. No doubt Comedy of Errors is the biggest horse that I have ever had through my hands. Terry Biddlecombe had left us and, in the twilight of his life as a jockey, was riding for Fulke Walwyn. For a brief period we took on Bill Smith, who was later to go to Fulke and become the Royal jockey, a position which he fills now with credit.

I always thought that Bill was a bit overhorsed on Comedy of Errors. He had had an upbringing in high-class show jumping and he sat up too much on his knees.

By the time that he was six years old, Comedy had proved himself to be the best hurdler in the country by winning the Champion Hurdle and the Welsh Champion Hurdle at Chepstow in his final two outings, beating the Northern crack Easby Abbey by a length at Cheltenham, and Bula, the dual champion, who was receiving 6 lb, by four lengths at Chepstow. He had earlier scored most impressively at Newcastle in the 'Fighting Fifth' Hurdle, in the Berkshire Hurdle at Newbury and at Nottingham.

Bill stayed with us at Kinnersley for two seasons and, although it was perhaps never the happiest of partnerships, he seized his chances. The first season he won the Champion on Comedy and rode our huge horse into second place behind Captain Christy in the Irish Sweeps Hurdle. The next season we won the Sweeps, but were beaten by Lanzarote in the Champion Hurdle. I have always blamed Bill for lying out of his ground. I think it was too much to let Lord Howard de Walden's horse, trained by Fred Winter, have so much leeway. You cannot give away ground. But, to give Bill his due, he says: 'The horse was just not right on the day. After three hurdles he couldn't go the pace. He couldn't get there. If he had been the same horse as he was in the Sweeps, he would have trotted up.'

Whatever the cause, this was a great shame. Comedy at his peak was a very great hurdler. He deserved to earn his place with the likes of Sir Ken and Persian War, who won the race that stamps the great champions three times. He was, in my opinion, superior to any of them and I can tell you this, Lanzarote would never have seen the way he went when he was at his best. There was no comparison between the two horses.

He won his second 'Fighting Fifth' and then, when Bill Smith left us and Ken White took over, Comedy had a fantastic season in 1974/75.

Starting off with the 'Fighting Fifth', he followed up with the

Cheltenham Trial Hurdle in December and then the Irish Sweeps on 27th December when he beat Lanzarote by a convincing length. That was a hat-trick, and he followed up with another, starting with Wolverhampton's Champion Hurdle Trial, the Champion Hurdle itself and finally the Scottish Champion Hurdle at Ayr.

This was the year when the going at Cheltenham was very heavy indeed. Gerry would have called it: 'Good jumping going.' But they don't think like that these days and there were even those who called themselves pundits and wrote in the papers: 'It was not fit to race.' I had never read such rubbish in my life. That is what jumping is all about. Why should races be cancelled, just because clerks of courses and executives are frightened of damaging their ground. There are a number of horses who, because of their low action, are suited to top of the ground conditions, of which we have have had more than our normal share in the last few years. It is totally unfair that the other horses should not have their chance: they have cost a lot of money to buy and keep, and their higher actions give them a disadvantage on top of the ground but an advantage in the soft or heavy. In the old days the mudlarks always came into their own at one stage or another. Now the tendency is for people to shut up shop as soon as the ground becomes at all heavy. Heaven knows, we have always been able to gallop through standing water if necessary. Those who cancel meetings because of unduly heavy going are, in my opinion, wet and stupid. Above all, they do not understand anything about horses. Why should they? Nowadays there are precious few of us who do and that includes a number of modern trainers.

As for those jockeys, who are constantly bleating at the first opportunity to the press: 'It really isn't fit to race.' Well, jumping isn't really a fit place for them. They should go back to their show jumping or their pony clubs or perhaps we could have a few races for them on the flat. National Hunt racing in these islands has always been a hard tough sport, and therein has lain its attraction. Long may it last. After all, steeplechasing is the one sport left at which Britain excels above all other nations in the world. This is because we are a nation of horsemen who understand the animals themselves, and because we still have a large number of people who have been reared in the tough school of the hunting field. It's easy enough to go prinking around the place, trying with no real hope of success to do a form of dressage and to follow this up with show jumping and cross-country riding. The real hunting man can do this, which is why, for so many years, Britain was in the forefront of eventing.

But we and our horses must remain tough, ready to take on the best in the world on any going. Those who are constantly trying to modify fences, making them easier, and to abandon meetings because of heavy going, have obviously never ridden steeplechasing themselves. Horses were the servants of man, who brought equitation and horsemanship to a fine art many years before the present members of the British Horse Society and the Pony Club, let alone the racing press and the clerks of courses, were even thought of. If all these people are allowed to have their way, we will end up like the Russians. And you saw what happened to them in the Grand National!

I say, make the fences that bit stiffer again, do not even think of abolishing the open ditch and race on heavy going. Only in this way will we remain the greatest steeplechasing nation.

Comedy of Errors is the perfect example of the saying, which I have mentioned before, that a top horse can remain at his peak for no more than three years. Until April 1977 he was still the highest prize-money winner of all time. He would have established an even higher record if he had won another Irish Sweeps Hurdle, but, on this occasion, there were enemy forces at work against the dual Sweeps and Champion winner. The bookmakers knew about it and one particular man was laying against our horse steadily taking money at longer odds than the others. So I was not surprised when Ken White and Comedy were viciously cut off on the home turn. The Leopardstown stewards acted and punished the culprit, but that did not give us the race, which we undoubtedly deserved. He was to go over the top fairly soon after. Mind, I am not all against bookmakers. Very much the opposite in fact. I like dealing with them and trying to beat the market. On the whole I usually manage to do so, but the tax has taken a lot of the value out of betting in the last few years and these days it is not possible for an owner to have a proper bet. I think there is one thing, however, against bookmakers today: we urgently need more money in the racing industry. Somehow, as in all other civilised countries, we, the professional racing people, who make our living out of the industry, the trainers, stable lads and so on, ought to benefit from this betting more than we do. I am not interested in politics. All I know is that British racing needs a lot more money desperately and deserves to get it. Bother all these so-called experts who are constantly shooting their mouths off. They think they know, but they don't. They are not actually in racing and only those who are appreciate the full force of the argument. If we can somehow achieve these two things while we still have bookmakers, then for heaven's sake, let's keep them. Even though they seem to be far more pinch-penny and mercenary since the big ones have become limited companies and no longer have any idea about regarding racing as sport, they still add to the variety.

Every year that the Irish Sweeps Hurdle has been run we have either won it or been placed. But now they have, misguidedly in my opinion, made it into a handicap. They expect to have thirty runners every time. Now this may be all right for the ordinary punters in Ireland, but not for the English, who do not know the strength of the Irish horses. They would always bet on a good race as it was before—a curtain raiser, if you like, for the Champion Hurdle. But I think they have made a grave mistake in giving that sort of prize money for a once a year handicap: you are in for trouble however good your exposed horse may be and bound to find that there is some animal down in the depths of Ireland, Surrey, Sligo or Sussex which has been specially cooked up for the last twelve months with this event in mind. They have made the race into a 'long handicap'.

Back in the autumn of 1976, just after the change had been announced, handicapper David Heyman asked me: 'What do you think of the conditions for the Irish Sweeps Hurdle?'

'I think it's bloody awful!' I replied.

We both agreed that people would be putting horses by just for that race and I said: 'I'm thinking of putting one by now to have it handicapped just right for Christmas 1977!'

Ken White's strength suited Comedy of Errors, who, after a fall in his first outing, was unbeaten in his remaining six races of the 1974/5 season. 'The Big Horse' as the Press called him, passed Arkle's prize winnings total and established himself as top British

National Hunt stakes winner of all time. Before the Champion Hurdle we showed Ken White over and over again the films of the previous year's race, when, ridden by Bill Smith, Comedy had been beaten by Lanzarote. We managed to instil in our jockey's mind that at all costs he must not lay out of his ground, but must lay up. We got our revenge over Fred Winter's horse very, very satisfactorily.

Comedy is not finished yet by any means, but he is perhaps not quite the strength that he used to be. I believe that if we had won that third Champion Hurdle and thereby joined the immortals, Persian War, Sir Ken and Hatton's Grace, he would deservedly have been hailed as the greatest hurdler of them all.

XI The Sting is in the Tail

With Ken White's impending retirement, we were joined by two new Irish jockeys, both former amateurs, John Burke and Sam Morshead. Both are good strong horsemen with excellent hands. I reckon myself lucky indeed to have them at Kinnersley.

But although I knew that we had some fair horses in the yard, the 1975/6 season started most disappointingly. It seemed that the horses were all wrong in themselves. With the help of our vet we left nothing to chance and, after exhaustive tests, cured some blood disorders.

Then I started to investigate the forage and after analysis discovered that the very finest oats, ripened and harvested in golden sunshine and imported from the other side of the world, are far lower in protein than the Racehorse Cubes marketed by Spillers. So half way through the season I switched. It is essential that the cubes should be absolutely freshly made. Otherwise the vitamins, which they contain, go off. You can tell when cubes are past their best because they become crumbly. So, before I changed, I stipulated that I must have a fresh load brought in to Kinnersley twice a week. One of the most important factors about feeding cubes is that you can guarantee complete consistency throughout the season.

Due I am sure to the cubes, which they love eating, our horses began to thrive and our fortunes changed dramatically for the better. We had bought a splendid young horse called Royal Frolic for Sir Edward Hanmer, and had trained him with the object of winning one special race, the Greenall Whitley Chase at Haydock, the favourite course of Sir Edward who at 86 was now unhappily in the twilight of his life. He especially wanted to win this important chase at the course where he had started as a steward nearly half a century earlier.

Royal Frolic duly obliged. He won twice at Wolverhampton and twice at Haydock, including the Greenall Whitley—in record time. Only a seven-year-old, he was obviously a fast improving chaser and the going in the spring of the driest year ever known in Britain was already right on top as we approached the National Hunt Festival at Cheltenham.

We entered Frolic for the Gold Cup, but he was an improbable runner until Mercy went racing on her own to Ascot. On her return, she said to me: 'I don't rate either Bula or What a Buck. We must run Frolic in the Gold Cup.' We discussed the matter and telephoned the Hanmers who, as always, agreed.

On Wednesday the ground was just too firm for Comedy's old legs. He seemed to feel the jarring in a way that he had not done when he was younger and that bit lighter. He finished fourth in the Champion Hurdle.

There was a little drama on that day. Jim Dreaper, who had trained Ten Up to win the previous year's Gold Cup in particularly heavy bog-like going, wanted to give the horse an injection before the race to prevent him from breaking blood vessels. Apparently he was allowed to do so in Ireland. But our stewards rightly decided that his action in using this injection could be considered a breach of the rules relating to doping.

The famous rule 200 states: 'Any person who administers or allows or causes to be administered or connives at the administration to a horse of a substance (other than a normal nutrient) which could alter its racing performance at the time of racing, shall be guilty of a breach of the Rules and may be declared a disqualified person or otherwise penalised by the stewards of the Jockey Club in the Jockey Club in accordance with their powers under Rules 2 of these Rules.'

As it happens, it would not have mattered on that going if Ten Up had been stuffed like a pin cushion full of every dope and anabolic steroid known to science. He still would not have won.

There were eleven runners for the classic of steeplechasing, the Piper Champagne Cheltenham Gold Cup chase run over three miles and a quarter and seventy-six yards, which this year was worth £18,134.50. to the winner. The firm of Piper Heidsieck had given £12,000 towards the race. They are particularly generous and hospitable to us at Cheltenham. I can do no better than allow

Len Thomas of *The Sporting Life* to tell the story of our second Gold Cup triumph.

Not since L'Escargot popped up at 33 to 1 seven years ago has there been a longer priced winner of the Gold Cup than Royal Frolic, who deservedly won the Piper Champagne sponsored race at Cheltenham yesterday.

Royal Frolic, owned by 86-year-old Sir Edward Hanmer and trained by Fred Rimell, was greeted by a stunned silence as he returned to be unsaddled.

He certainly deserved better than this as he battled every yard of the way in the hands of John Burke to win from the Irish challengers and stable companions Brown Lad and Colebridge.

The Kinnersley horse, along with Roman Bar the youngest in the field, thus followed in the footsteps of Woodland Venture, whom Rimell saddled to win this race back in 1967.

So Jim Dreaper, who trained Ten Up to win the corresponding event last year, saddled the second and third, but was annoyed that he had to withdraw Ten Up.

It seems to me there must be closer standardisation of the rules of the Irish Turf Club and our own, which in my opinion, were correctly interpreted by the stewards.

Royal Frolic was bought by Rimell on behalf of Sir Edward with one race in mind—the Greenall Whitley Chase at Haydock, which he proceeded to win.

After that Rimell suggested to Sir Edward that the horse should be entered for the Gold Cup, but the latter remarked: 'I don't know. He seems a bit young.'

Rimell replied diplomatically: 'Well none of us are getting any younger and I think he should take his chance.'

So Sir Edward agreed and Mrs Rimell promptly bet a fiver each way at 500 to 1. So there was certainly one happy person as Royal Frolic returned to the winner's enclosure! It was not a particularly strong pace in the early stages, Money Market and What A Buck cutting out the work followed by Glanford Brigg and The Dikler.

There was no appreciable change going out on the final circuit, other than Royal Frolic moving past The Dikler into fourth place.

Glanford Brigg took over shortly before racing up the hill, chased by Colebridge, with Royal Frolic, What A Buck and The Dikler close behind.

Running down to the third last, Glanford Brigg was in front but coming to the fence Royal Frolic was in the air first. The seven-year-old then quickly went ahead but by now Brown Lad who was totally ill at ease on the ground, Colebridge and Bula, last in the early stages, were poised to challenge.

Bula made a complete hash of the third last and that quickly put paid to his chance, so it was left to Brown Lad and Colebridge to fight it out with the leader.

But Royal Frolic, jumping superbly, had no intention of surrendering his advantage and taking the last in grand style, strode up the hill to pass the post with five lengths to spare.

Colebridge, who now goes for the Grand National, was a similar distance away third, followed by Money Market, also an Aintree probable, Glanford Brigg and Bula.

John Francome had no excuses for Bula other than saying: 'His running was too bad to be true.'

Fred Winter, who trains the horse said: 'He ran a bad race. I have no idea why, but horses are unpredictable. I thought he was as well as I could get him, but somehow I felt on the journey here that he wouldn't win. I've got a feeling about this race—like Gordon Richards had about the Derby.'

The Gold Cup has been a real bogey for Winter, the luckless defeat of Pendil by the Dikler here three years ago being a case in point.

Well, I hate to remind my old pal, but Mercy had that same feeling about Bula when she saw him run at Ascot. Which after all was why we ran Frolic!

Incidentally, I have now a very promising shooting dog who has been honoured with the name of Frolic.

We were not finished yet. There was still the Grand National to come. Some time earlier we had been sent a big chestnut chaser called Rag Trade by 'Teasie Weasie' Raymond, the famous flamboyant hairdresser.

We had some anxious moments in the run up to the Grand National. As I said, Rag Trade is a big heavy clumsy type of horse, who hits the ground fairly hard and the prevailing ground now was on top. After Chepstow and his victory in the Welsh Grand National he developed heat in his off foreleg, which was there in the evening but gone by morning and which did not seem to affect him. Raymond, whom we had not worried with this, had refrained from backing his horse heavily because he was frightened that Rag Trade would not be at his best on the fast ground that we would inevitably find at Liverpool. However, the night before, our old friend and his former trainer, Keith Piggott, telephoned to tell him that he agreed with us and that Rag Trade would act very well on the Aintree ground. So Raymond had his bet and the horse started at 14 to 1.

That Saturday 3rd April 1976 at Liverpool was a great day all round for us. It started particularly happily when old Comedy of Errors, ridden by Ken White, gave 3 lb and a short head beating in the Templegate Hurdle to the crack New Zealand six-year-old Grand Canyon, who was to win the famous international Colonial Cup at Camden, South Carolina, later in the year.

This was the first year that Ladbroke's had taken over Aintree and there had been a great deal of razzamatazz throughout the meeting. The Grand National, sponsored to the tune of £40,000 by the *News of the World*, was worth £37,420 to the winner. Barona was favourite and Red Rum, bidding for his third National was second favourite at 10 to 1. I always thought him lucky to win the first time. Far too much use was made of that brave Australian horse Crisp, who was giving him 23 lb and was beaten only three parts of a length in a time that was 19 seconds faster than Golden Miller's record.

But now it was our turn to set up records.

John Burke rode a blinder. He came into the last nicely poised behind Eyecatcher and Red Rum, who took the fence together. He collected Rag Trade, balanced him and drove him up to the leaders. At the elbow on that long run-in he was fractionally in front of Red Rum and our horse ran on splendidly to win by two lengths. No one can deny that Rag Trade fully deserved his success. As a result I became the first trainer to send out four Aintree Grand National winners. What is more I was the first man to win the Cheltenham Gold Cup and the National in the same season since Vincent O'Brien did so with Knock Hard and Early

Mist in 1953. And, as they were ridden by Tim Molony and Bryan Marshall respectively, John Burke became the first man to have won both races on different horses for the same trainer in the same year.

I buy quite a few unbroken horses and reckon to take six weeks to break them. My head man, Ron Peachey, is very good at breaking and drives a horse well on long reins.

As with everything in training, so much depends on the individual as to how long it takes before breaking him and giving him his first run. Our last Gold Cup winner, Royal Frolic, example, for had his first run six months after he was backed. Then we put him by for a year. If I have a horse that may be short of a race before the Grand National, I might work him over two and half miles but normally I never work him over further than a mile and a half and, if I want to ask him a question, it is never over further than a mile and a quarter. Between his races the average horse will just keep cantering nicely and then four days before his race I give him a mile and a quarter gallop just to blow him out. That is for a horse that is fit and ready. I don't believe in giving a horse a pipe-opener on the day before a race like most trainers unless he is a stuffy sort.

Although there was no party afterwards, we came home to a tremendous reception at Kinnersley and Sunday morning all the locals were out in force at Severn Stoke to salute a great National winner when Mercy and I took Rag Trade along for them to see. There's no place like home. And once again we were at the top of the trainers' list with a new record total of over £110,000.

I school less than anybody. Just the beginning of the season. I never school again unless the horse has a fall and needs his mind refreshing. And then, by and large, I put him in the loose school. It is important not to over-school. You have to give your horse confidence in the same way as you'd treat a human being. If he has confidence he will attack his fences or hurdles with zest and enthusiasm whereas, if you overschool him he will get soured up and careless.

When Comedy of Errors fell over hurdles I was constantly being asked: 'Have you schooled him since he fell?'

I said the same thing every time. 'Let the bugger remember that fall. He won't be inclined to do it again. What good is a school over three little hurdles going to do?' All the people who should know better, the so-called pundits, seem to make the same mistake. John Oaksey asked me the other day whether I had schooled Zarib after his fall. Once again I said: 'No. I want him to remember.'

Of course if you know that you have a cowardly horse who is apt to put on the brakes and he falls, that is a different matter. Then you would give him a jump. You must know your horse's character, and then you will know when to school and when not to. Remember, every time that you school a horse, there is a distinct chance that he might jump into himself or another horse might jump into him.

Sometimes you have a horse that is sticky. I have one now called Breeze Wagon. He has to be schooled quite a lot. He gets so sticky that three days before he is going to run he is put back in the loose school for a reminder. There are four hurdles in the school. So, if he goes round there four times he's jumped sixteen hurdles. He's going to learn something one way or the other!

There are as many different variations as there are different characters. Some horses will yield to one treatment and some to another. For some horses hunting is the finest thing you can do. For a horse to hunt he ought to be a tough character or possibly a horse that has been soured of racing. It gives him a new outlook in an entirely fresh environment. But today you can get into so much trouble in the hunting field. You can get your horse into wire, kicked, staked or caught in a hole. It's a fairly hazardous operation if you have a horse that you think is fairly valuable.

When our horses finish racing we prefer either to retire them here at Kinnersley or to have them put down, unless we are very sure where they are going to. Because, if a horse has been in training as a racehorse, he has obviously been extremely well-looked-after and we have given him the best of everything. It is really rather cruel to fling him suddenly into the yard of a one-horse owner, who may be tremendously enthusiastic but has not a clue about true horsemastership and looking after top-class thoroughbreds. The horse then almost inevitably deteriorates and has a horrid life. We would much rather have him put down.

I'm a little worried about the standard of training among some of the younger generation. A lot of the young boys who have come into the profession recently really have very little background training in it. I asked a well known jockey the other day what he was going to do when he stopped riding. He said: 'I'm going to train.'

I said: 'Well, as you never served your time, you ought to spend at least a year in a top-class stable, to learn something about it.'

He replied: 'Oh no, I'll get a good head man.'

To which I replied somewhat naturally I think: 'How on earth will you know that you've got a good head man when you don't know anything about the job yourself?'

Now take another of our Aintree horses, Brown Admiral, he is always a stuffy individual—in fact he is the stuffiest of all our forty-eight horses at Kinnersley. He has to be galloped properly twice a week. He would suit certain trainers I could name, particularly at Epsom, very well! He would be the ideal horse for those who insist on galloping their horses flat out twice a week to try them. But out of all our forty-eight horses he would be the only one who would thrive on it because nowadays the horses like that are so few and far between. There is no doubt that the horses of today are nothing like as strong and tough as they were when my father was training here before the war. We had to give them far longer and more strenuous exercise.

Incidentally I think that the Jockey Club's new find in the analysis and detection of anabolic steroids is going to make a big difference in the immediate future. After what has been happening you would not have anything to do with a French horse at any rate unless you had had a saliva test first.

A Ruby Wedding. No less. Mercy and I look back this year on forty years of marriage and the partnership which was formed then is stronger than ever. We are satisfied with our life.

Mercy's father was mad on hunting and rode a lot of point-to-point winners. She and her brother rode as soon as they could walk and her brother, a committee member and a stalwart of the Warwickshire Hounds, still hunts four days a week.

Both our children have ridden winners. Scarlett was champion at the International Horse Show at the White City two years running on a 12 hand pony called Peter Pan. She won with it at Richmond and Windsor too. And then she rode a lot of point-to-point winners. Guy, despite his height, also rode several point-to-point winners and when he was seventeen he won the only hunter chase in which he ever rode. The race was at Wincanton and the horse had been bred by Mercy's father, who had given it to Guy.

As professionals, we particularly dislike the sort of ultra horsey women who are firmly convinced that they have invented it all and are unhappily becoming more and more common in the horse world today. They do not know and their constant criticism of everyone is annoying in the extreme. One particular lady of this type who can only be described as a bitch, is always saying something horrid about everybody else. She received her 'comeuppance' on the day when she came up to Mercy with her teeth clacking as usual and really riled her.

Said Mercy: 'Everyone in our family has ridden winners either under Rules or in point-to-points—all four of us. Have you, madam, ever ridden a point-to-point winner, as you are so very knowledgeable?' Of course the answer inevitably was no!

We are grandparents. Both our children married soon. Guy was wedded to Mary, the daughter of Jaguar's chief, Sir William Lyons, and Scarlett to Robin Knipe, a hunting farmer and an outstanding amateur until his riding career was cut short by a horrible accident, from which at one time we doubted whether he would fully recover. Happily he has done so and he and Scarlett now run a stud at their home with some fair stallions. During our summer break Mercy and I have been on safari to Africa several times.

Buffaloes are often mean devils; if you don't get them they will get you. You have to pay a £100 for a licence to shoot a buffalo, two elan, some plains game and a few odds and ends. So you do not usually shoot too many of them. I had a very narrow escape one day.

We had walked for about two miles after a herd of buffalo when one of the gun bearers came up and said: 'There are three or four in a bit of swamp over there.'

We stalked round to the right side of them and walked to within fifty yards. You could only just see the shadows of them by a tree and one of the bearers said: 'We will stand here and wait because he will come and have a look at us with a bit of luck.'

Suddenly he said: 'Are you ready? Because I think he's coming.'

With that, down went the buffalo's head and in he came charging hard at us. I got him in the chest and the White hunter hit him in the bottom of the jaw. Still he came on and I was thinking that our shots hadn't stopped him when suddenly he went down, slithered along the ground and finished up only fifteen yards from us. I turned round and saw one of the little black boys had shinned up a tree. He was stuck up there petrified. The trees were not very strong and I thought he might come down at any moment. I asked: 'What's he doing up there?'

The white hunter laughed. 'If you'd been out here as long as him, you'd be up the tree too.'

I said: 'The damn thing wouldn't hold me!'

We are in the breeding business too. At the end of 1973 our old friend and owner Tony Dillon bought the Longfield Stud in County Tipperary, with 193 acres of that wonderful Tipperary pasture land on which so many great winners have been reared over the years. For some years it belonged to Vincent O'Brien whose celebrated Ballydoyle training establishment is over on the other side of Cashel. At Longfield Vincent stood his first Irish Derby winner Chamier, and also that lovely quality horse Hugh Lupus, sire of the St Leger winner Hethersett, who in turn produced the Epsom winner Blakeney, now such a tremendous success at our National Stud.

As he acquired more land and was able to enlarge the property at Ballydoyle, Vincent sold Longfield. It was run as a farm for four years until Tony bought it. With Tony's tremendous enthusiasm and financial backing we have spared no effort to rebuild Longfield. Tony has announced his intention of making it one of the finest and most important studs in Ireland. He has taken me into partnership with him.

After extensive building, rebuilding and fencing, we are now well on the way to achieving Tony's aim. We are lucky to have as our resident manager Sue Francis, the attractive daughter of our old friend Cheshire trainer Doug and niece of Devon Loch's jockey, the celebrated novelist Dick Francis.

At present we are standing three decent stallions, Martinmas, Take a Reef and Quayside. We are always on the look-out for better and better horses. Although he now lives in Jersey Tony's great hope is that he will breed top class jumpers at Longfield. But meanwhile our stallions continue to get an increasing number of good flat race winners.

Running the stud and all that it entails is extremely relaxing work for Mercy and me. We visit our lovely stud regularly. But even when I do retire, I will never move to Ireland. I am much too fond of Worcestershire and of British racing. On the other hand, wouldn't it be wonderful for us to round it all off by breeding our own winner of the Grand National?

I really thought that we were going to increase our record to five Grand Nationals until Andy Pandy, full of running and looking a certain winner, just failed to lower his undercarriage in time as he landed over Becher's in the lead, second time round.

However, he made handsome amends by winning the Whitbread Gold Cup at Sandown and, as long as the handicapper treats us fairly, it will surely take a good one to beat him at Aintree in 1978 and give the Rimells a nap hand.

Index

Index